...NISTRY

Thank you for your generous support!

...ruly appreciate your partnership in this Great ...mmandment and Great Commission ministry.

Please sign me up for email updates:

☒ _____

Please use my gift for:

☐ Where Most Needed   ☐ International Staff Support

☐ Biblical Leadership Training Centers   ☐ US Staff Support

☐ Global Church Relief   ☐ Bible Distribution

If you have any questions, please email Jake at **Jake@leadershipintl.org.**

CJ DAVISON

MW010949.2

"Next Gen Leaders cannot afford to go it alone. Missional friendship, grounded in Triune Love and abiding in Christ as our closest companion, can transform how we make disciples of all nations. And yet, this essential, everyday theme is overlooked. Through a beautiful fusion of personal stories, practicing what he preaches, and deep biblical reflection on the fruitful life, CJ leads us back into the beating heart of mission. May we follow him there."

-DR DAVE BENSON
Director of the Centre for Culture and Discipleship with
The London Institute for Contemporary Christianity

"In a generation that is increasingly interconnected, CJ has rightly identified something as foundational as friendships as an essential and enjoyable part of life, discipleship and ministry in the kingdom, crucial in compelling us toward the mission of God in our lifetime."

-JOSH YEOH
Founder of Penang House of Prayer and Worship
Leader at Riverlife Church in Singapore

"What a treat to read this book! It was an eye opener and incredibly refreshing. It gave words and framework to a core conviction in our life and ministry: missional friendships. This book is full of life-transforming truths. CJ Davison not only unpacked his deep wisdom on the matter, but is also someone who walks the talk."

-SARAH AND RENÉ BREUEL
Sarah Breuel, Revive Europe Director and Evangelism Training
Coordinator IFES Europe. René Breuel, Church Planter and Author

MISSIONAL FRIENDSHIPS

MISSIONAL FRIENDSHIPS

JESUS' DESIGN FOR FRUITFUL LIFE AND MINISTRY

CJ DAVISON

 ACOMA PRESS

For my family and friends whom the Lord has graciously provided.

TABLE OF CONTENTS

FORWARD

In his gospel, Matthew records for us that at the beginning of His ministry, Jesus moved to live in Capernaum by the sea, in the territory of Zebulun and Naphtali. While walking by the Sea of Galilee, he saw two brothers, Simon and Andrew busily at work as fishermen, and said to them, "...Follow me, and I will make you fishers of men" (Matt. 4:19b).

On Jesus' very last night with the anxious and questioning disciples, John records for us Jesus' deeply assuring and comforting words to them, "but I have called you friends" (John 15:15). This relational inclusio in the life and ministry of Jesus calls every follower to focus attention on the most important truth for fruitful Christian living and service: "abide in me and I in you ... for apart from me you can do nothing" (John 15:4a, 5b).

In the frenzied busyness of life in our global village and frantic search for quick-fix solutions today, many good things easily distract our attention. We must regain our focus on abiding relationship with Jesus, friendships with others who are doing the same and ministry that flows out of these friendships.

In *Missional Friendships*, CJ Davison gives us a timely reminder of the urgency of this need. Davison shares his concern and observations, such as this one, "I never had a discussion on friendship in seminary and the word is missing in many systematic theology books" (page 15). My own seminary surprise while studying missions came when I learned that 86% of Muslims, Buddhists and Hindus globally do not know any Christian in person – what a challenge to our faith conviction and missional commitment!

As we celebrate the dynamic growth of the Church into the future in new regions of the global southeast regions, the call for Christ-centered friends will become even more urgent. World Christianity professor and leading historian Dana L. Robert tells of a memorable moment during the

World Missionary Conference at Edinburgh in 1910 when V. S. Azariah, a young, newly ordained Anglican from South India gave the heartfelt cry "you have given your goods to feed the poor. You have given your bodies to be burned. We also ask for *love*. Give us FRIENDS![1]" Robert further reflects that a key that unlocks the history of missions from the 1910 World Missionary Conference to the mid-twentieth century is that of cross-cultural friendships. She warns that Christian community depends upon personal relationships, and missionary failures can be traced to the lack of such relationships.[2]

After His resurrection, Jesus solemnly charged His disciples, "...As the Father has sent me, even so I am sending you." (John 20:21b).

Should we do anything otherwise? God's friendship with us in the incarnation is in itself deeply instructive for our fruitful abiding and obedient following of Christ. Read *Missional Friendships* prayerfully through the three well-structured sections of the book, paying attention to the burden of the author's heart with his invitation, "I hope you understand how important friendship is for the work God calls us to."

Nana Yaw Offei Awuku, May 2020
Global Associate Director for Generations
Lausanne Movement
Accra, Ghana

INTRODUCTION

Missing the Forest for the Trees

Sometimes we miss the forest for the trees. We get so focused on the details that we miss the obvious. We live in a busy world with urgent demands and sometimes the "fires" keep us so focused on the trees that we rarely look up and see the forest around us.

Friendship is one of the forests we have missed. We have made life and ministry so complicated and missed the importance of friendship with God and the people He has made.

When I think about the value of friendship, I think about my grandfather. He lived in a small town in Vermont where he knew most of his town. He used to say, "Treat everyone like your best friend." For him it was a practical strategy for life. Though he lived in a world far different from mine, I think my grandpa was on to something profound.

For such a basic concept, the Church has often neglected (or taken for granted) the study of and practice of Christ-like friendship. At best, sermons may touch on the friendship of Jonathan and David (1 Sam. 18:1-4). I never had a discussion on friendship in seminary and the topic is only briefly discussed in my systematic theology book.

Yet, I fully believe that if future Christian leaders are going to be effective in life and ministry, we need to step back and see the friendship forest. So, let me briefly share three reasons why friendship deserves more attention.

1. Friendship brings spiritual growth

Who are the people that have impacted you the most? The answer is, most likely, your friends. Relationships change people. The closer we are to people, the more they change us. That is why we need to see friendship as a crucial and necessary part of our sanctification. Godly friendships can make us more like Jesus. The disciples' interactions with each other sharpened, encouraged and challenged each other to be more godly during and after their time with Christ on earth. Similarly, the closer we grow in friendship with God, the more we become like Him. As we will see, Jesus' friendship with His disciples is a prime example of a relationship that forever changed the disciples' hearts and minds.

2. Discipleship requires friendship

Did Jesus make disciples or friends? We will find that these terms are not mutually exclusive. Discipleship is a popular term these days and rightly so, as it is at the core of Jesus' ministry and command to us (Matt. 28:19-20). Yet in the Bible we find that Jesus called His disciples friends for a very specific reason. If we want to follow Jesus, we must imitate His friendship-making discipleship strategy.

3. Friendship is a ministry tool

Why do you have the friends you have? Likely it is because you share something in common. The more important the common interest, the closer you will be. God and His mission are of utmost value. So, in light of this reality, we should find the strongest relationships in local churches and ministries where people serve together. There are opportunities all around us to make and use friendships as a tool to serve God and others. The pattern we see in Scripture is that friendship with Jesus leads to transforming friendships with others, which leads to fruit-producing ministry.

Will you explore God's heart for friendship?

I hope that as you read this book, you will get a glimpse of God's beautiful heart for relationships, intimacy and friendship. With John 13-17 as our guide, we will see that our role in God's story is to bear fruit for His glory. The ingredients for this fruit-bearing includes a **foundation** with Jesus, requires **friendship** with others and compels us to then **focus** on His mission together.

In section one, we will see why relationships are God's strategy and how we relate to God in friendship through abiding. In section two, we will look at the idea of missional friendships and our crucial role of reaching people with the life-giving relationship that Jesus shares with us. In section three, we will look at how missional friendships form the building blocks for the bigger kingdom goals of collaboration and unity.

SECTION 1

Fruitful Foundations:
Friendship with Jesus

Jesus: Our Map, Mission and Motivation

My Ghanaian friend Nana says that in Africa a person's last words are extremely important. They are esteemed above other words as if the soul is pouring out profound truths for the remembrance and honor of the life lived. Perhaps you still cherish the last words of a friend or loved one who has passed.

We should treat Jesus' "last" words with the same respect and reflection. Before He died, Jesus shared a Passover meal with His closest disciples. This Last Supper conversation was emotional, intimate and strategic. Jesus shared a ministry-shaping and life-giving message that shaped the future of the disciples' lives. It should shape us too if we heed His words. As we examine John 13-17, I would encourage you to study it yourself. Don't just take my word for it. I hope you see for yourself Jesus' beautiful design for life and ministry.

When the disciples came to their Passover meal with Jesus, they were unaware of the imminent betrayal and crucifixion. Jesus, knowing what lay ahead, carefully used the remaining time before His death to share His heart and plans. It is no coincidence that these words come around the Last Supper and Jesus' invitation to a new covenant.

The disciples grew concerned when Jesus said He was going away (John 13:33). The disciples had been with Jesus, loved following Him, and now it seemed they would continue "alone," while Jesus went to prepare a place for them (John 14:3). The idea of losing their Master was unnerving. Simon Peter asked, "Lord, where are you going?" (John 13:36) and Thomas asked "How can we know the way?" (John 14:5). They were asking in a practical sense about a path on earth to be with Jesus.

We see the disciples' confusion in one of the questions they asked, "Judas (not Iscariot) said to Him, 'Lord, how is it that you will manifest yourself to us, and not to the world?'" John 14:22. How could Jesus leave, be near His disciples, and not be seen by the world at the same time? Fortunately, since it concerns us too, Jesus was not quiet on this topic. He lovingly gave several clear messages:

- Jesus would continue working (John 14:6, 13-14).
- He was not leaving to stop the work, but rather to increase the work (John 14:12).
- The disciples would not be alone (John 14:16-21, 28).
- The disciples would live through Him (John 14:19).
- Jesus would manifest Himself to His beloved (John 14:21).
- Jesus was going ahead more than going away (John 13:36).
- The mode would change but the mission was the same. Jesus would send the Spirit to help and be with them (John 14:16-17, 25-26).

Jesus made it clear that His plan was to continue ministry on earth with and through His disciples (Matt. 28:18-20). This begs several questions: What is God's plan? Why is He doing it this way and what should we do? We find an important part of that answer in John 14:6-7 when Jesus said, "Jesus said to him, 'I am the way, and the truth, and the life. No one comes to the Father except through me. If you had known me, you would have known my Father also. From now on you do know him and have seen him.'"

The answer is both simple and profound. Jesus is the way to the Father. To know Jesus is to know the Father and to know the Father is eternal life (John 17:3). This means that God's plan is primarily relational. The strategy is relational and the end result is relationship with God. This is not a future plan. The plan is current and active for all disciples on earth. We know that because eternal life begins here and now in relationship with God. We may be waiting for redeemed bodies, but we are not waiting to know God. Therefore, this grand relational redemption strategy is working its way through creation as we speak. And, if that is true, then there is significant work to be done and our lives have incredible meaning and significance on earth.

John 14:6 is often used as a text about personal salvation, but we need to see it as more than that. Jesus was not simply sharing a personal salvation plan for His disciples, though it includes that. Jesus was sharing a foundational truth to direct and guide His disciples for life and ministry (John 14:12-14). If Jesus is the way, truth and life, then all redemptive ministry must be in and through Jesus because the end goal is knowing God. Jesus' words are a relational invitation to know Him and walk with Him now. This leads us to two practical implications about ministry. First, ministry is impossible without Jesus. Second, to do ministry requires knowing and working with Jesus.

We know this is foundational to Jesus' strategy for life and ministry because He was preparing His disciples for ministry after He left earth. His words were not meant to dissuade the disciples from doing ministry. It was quite the opposite. Their journey was not ending with His death, resurrection and ascension, but it was going to change significantly and it started with knowing the Way, Truth and Life.

Jesus' plan to leave and work through His disciples was a good and necessary change for greater effectiveness. Jesus said, "Truly, truly, I say to you, whoever believes in me will also do the works that I do; and greater works than these will he do, because I am going to the Father" (John 14:12). Since the work would still be primarily Jesus', the disciples could and would participate by asking in His name (John 14:13-14).

We cannot ignore the raw simplicity and implications of Jesus' statements. This was a forest moment and Jesus set a clear course for the disciples. If Jesus' presence and authority were necessary for the first disciples, then it is certainly true for us and this topic deserves renewed attention. So, let us dive deeper into the implications of life and ministry Jesus, our mission (way), map (truth) and motivation (life).

Mission: where are we going?

I was fortunate to take a short flight to view Mount Everest from the sky. The beauty of the mountain is hard to describe and it was an event I will not forget. Mount Everest stood far above everything around it, even the clouds. It was a spectacular sight as our plane rose above the clouds and got a glimpse of the peak at over 29,000 feet. Even from the plane, it was absolutely unimaginable to grasp the magnitude of the mountain.

Perhaps the disciples felt the same way when Jesus commanded them to make disciples of all nations (Matt. 28:19). Perhaps they felt as if they were at the bottom of a gigantic, even impossible, task ahead of them like climbing Mt. Everest. I believe many Christians feel the same way today, looking at the state of the world and the distance between here and making disciples in every ethnic group. It seems a long way up!

Many people have tried to summit Everest and failed. Some have died trying. Some have given up. Some never started. However, I guarantee that no one wandered to the top. No one ended up at the summit by accident. Before anyone stood on top, it was a vision and a mission with a plan.

We need not be overwhelmed because Jesus' mission comes with a vision and plan. But we need a fresh perspective, not from the base, but from the clouds. The prophet Habakkuk's vision is that one day the whole earth will be filled with the knowledge of the glory of God (Hab. 2:14). Jesus will be glorified, lifted up for all to see, far higher than Mount Everest.

Reaching the summit requires making disciples of all nations, but the mountain itself is not a task. The mountain, God's presence and glory, is already present and available. God is already working for His glory (John 13:31-32, 17:1-5) and Jesus has already gone before us and showed the way. The remaining work is not to create the mountain or build a path. We are simply called to reveal Him (John 14:13, 15:8, 17:22-23), meaning that our service is a joyful journey more than an impossible trek.

Map: who made yours?

When I was a young teenager, I went on a 10-day camping trip with the Boy Scouts. I was one of the youngest in the group, which included my father and older brother. At different points, we took turns leading the group. About halfway through the trip, my turn had come.

As we started hiking, everyone followed behind me. It was a great feeling for a young man! At first, everything went well. It seemed easy: follow the map and remember where north and south were. Unfortunately, I remained confident despite some obvious problems that arose. After a while, the path got less and less clear. Eventually we were hacking through bushes and straining to find the faint path. It was looking like we were lost and people started to question my leadership and direction. We stopped to have a frank conversation about the situation.

I was adamant that I was right and we were exactly where we were supposed to be. Others were less confident. We argued. I pointed to the map as my source of confidence and we carried on. In reality, we continued to be off track and barely found our way to the destination. When we finally arrived, people were upset and tired from hacking through overgrown bushes. Needless to say, I did not lead the group again.

What we found out later is that I had used the wrong map. I was given a park map, but it was an old one. It was outdated and the paths had changed since the map was published. Someone had given me the wrong map. The destination was not necessarily the problem, the map was.

Following the right map makes all the difference for where we end up. The path matters and the right map can mean life or death for those we lead. We have seen this in our churches and ministries. Sometimes we follow predictable patterns from outdated worldly maps. We walk along the ruts created by generations before us and, before long, we have gone so far down the wrong path that we cannot imagine a better way.

Jesus is the truth (John 4:6) in whom we can trust to lead us well. As David said, "Make me to know your ways, O LORD; teach me your paths. Lead me in your truth and teach me, for you are the God of my salvation; for you I wait all the day long" (Ps. 25:4-5). For those in Christ, we do not need to search for a faint path, we have the True Map with us and He will never lead us astray.

Motivation: your "why" leaks out

You can have the right map and mission, but if your heart is not in it, you may not make it. It is hard to summit Mount Everest without a passion for it. Half-hearted efforts may work with small tasks, but feats like climbing the tallest mountain in the world require a pressing conviction inside us.

Our core convictions reveal our "why." Why are you in ministry? The answer to that will illuminate the deep-seated values and longings of your heart. Sometimes those values stay hidden for a long time, but they eventually surface, for good or worse, in times of difficulty, struggle or friction. As David wisely said, "And see if there be any grievous way in me, and lead me in the way everlasting!" (Ps. 139:24).

People learn how to conceal their "why," but it usually comes out like a leaky faucet or worse, a volcano. We have all seen people's "why" leak out in moments of lapse or collapse, usually revealing a desire for money, sexual pleasure or power. As Christians, we need to inspect our "why" before the magma beneath the crust threatens to explode out of us. Without God's intervention, even disciples naturally shift towards selfishness and false idols. We may be walking with Jesus, but all along we make it about ourselves, glorifying ourselves instead of Him. To change, we need Jesus, the Life, to motivate and move us on mission.

Several years ago, the president of a large ministry allowed me to come and spend time with him. His message was simple, "Be careful." Many successful and well-known leaders are no longer in ministry because of moral failures. Most of the time it is not a competence issue; it is a heart issue. Strategies are good, but we need to get our hearts right.

I have seen it firsthand. Hurricane Irma came through the Turks and Caicos Islands in 2017 and devastated part of the Caribbean. I came shortly after the hurricane to help equip local pastors to respond to the disaster, providing relief supplies as an opportunity to show and share the Gospel. My colleague and I organized a training for dozens of churches on the main island of Turks and Caicos. We taught about the character of God, why He allows suffering and how suffering can lead people to a suffering Savior. Then we distributed supplies to the leaders in preparation for an island-wide distribution at their local churches for the most needy in the community. Radio stations announced the distribution sites to prepare people to come and get much-needed supplies like tarps, flashlights and blankets. What made the situation around the distribution timely, and tense, is that there was another hurricane (Matthew) headed towards the island.

After training the pastors, we thought it was clear that the distributions were designed to reach the lost and needy in the community with the love of God. The next day, my colleague and I visited the church distributions. Some were chaotic, with hundreds of people in line waiting for hours. For the most part, people were being served and seeing the body of Christ at work. However, as we came to one church in particular, we could tell something was wrong. There was a mob, not a line, outside the church with people angrily banging on the door.

We cautiously pushed through the crowd, went in and asked for the pastor. He was standing at the back of the church in front of a door, stunned.

"Where are the supplies?" We asked.

"Behind me, in this room." The pastor answered.

"Can we see them?" My colleague and I inquired.

When the door opened, it took just a second to realize there were not many supplies left.

"Where did the supplies go?" We asked.

The pastor did not give a straight answer. After prodding more, we found out that the pastor had privately given most of the supplies to his friends and family, not the needy and most vulnerable. We were mad and he was scared. He knew the desperate community needed the supplies, and there was not enough left for the mob.

By then the crowd had gotten through the doors and inside the church. We were up against a wall, literally, in between needy people and supplies they desperately needed. We called for police backup to come and control the growing crowd pressing in towards us. At that time, I turned to the pastor and pleaded with him to say something to calm the crowd and help people understand the situation. I will never forget his response, "These are not my people."

His true intentions had just leaked out. I could see it in his eyes and hear it in his voice. The hungry, needy crowd was not his concern. "His people" had already been taken care of but "these people" were of no matter to him.

My heart sank and then I realized we still had an irritated crowd in front of us, who had pushed their way inside the building. I knew the police were not going to get there quickly, so I closed my eyes and prayed for God to help. As I looked up, there were two gigantic strong men, a head above everyone else, pushing the crowds away from us. To this day, I do not know who they were. I have to think they were prompted by the Spirit or angels directly sent from God, because everyone moved as they pushed all the people away towards the front door.

The police finally came. They could not calm the crowd, but they did help us take out the remaining supplies and relocate the distribution across town safely. As we were leaving, we stumbled upon another room, which the church tried to hide from us. Some of the most valuable supplies, like flashlights and bug spray, given to the church for the most vulnerable in the community were being hidden from the community. As we gathered the remaining supplies and left the church, the police turned and said, "This is a disgrace."

I will not forget the feeling of utter disappointment I experienced that day. How did the angry crowd perceive the church that day? It was a far cry from how Christ interacted with hungry crowds and needy people.

Our motivation matters because we stand between a needy world and the precious love of Christ. If we are willing, we can share it with the world. But if we are only pursuing personal gain, we not only risk our ministry, we risk leading the world further away from the One they truly need.

Our motivation for life and ministry must be Christ alone. When the crowds began to leave Jesus, He turned to His disciples to ask them if they would also leave. Simon Peter profoundly responded, "'Lord, to whom shall we go? You have the words of eternal life, and we have believed, and have come to know, that you are the Holy One of God'" (John 6:68b-69). In other words, how can we not follow you?

When Christ is our motivation, a life of ministry flows from communion with our Savior. Even courageous ministry is possible because of the overflow of Life in us. I think of David when he first heard the taunts of Goliath. The Israelite army was scared frozen even though King Saul offered a reward for standing up to this enemy. Apparently, Saul's motivation was not enough because none took up the challenge! Israel's "why" left them with no strength to fight their enemy.

When David came, he had no interest in King Saul's offer of monetary gain or fame. David was instigated to take on the giant after hearing Goliath's taunts against God and His people. David took his stance boldly, "Then David said to the Philistine, 'You come to me with a sword and with a spear and with a javelin, but I come to you in the name of the LORD of hosts, the God of the armies of Israel, whom you have defied'" (1 Sam. 17:45). David confidently tells Goliath that he will win so, "... that all the earth may know that there is a God in Israel," (1 Sam. 17:46b). David's motivation was for God's name to be exalted. That is a "why" worth living for!

> *"...your name and remembrance are the desire of our soul."*
> Isaiah 26:8b

Who is getting the glory?

When my son was two, he wanted to imitate everything I did, from the words I used and the food I ate to the way I brushed my teeth and talked to his mother. I even heard him calling my wife "babe!"

One time, my son asked to help me take out the trash. Of course, I was delighted that he wanted to help, but unsure how he could. Nevertheless, he wanted to help so I called him over and we proceeded to the kitchen trash bin together. I realized quickly that the trash bag was too heavy for him to lift, so I took it out of the bin. We walked together to the front door and I asked him to open it. He tried, but could not fully, so I opened it with him. Then we walked outside to the side gate. The side gate is tricky to open, so I unlocked it as he stood and watched. I opened it a bit and asked him to pull it all the way open. He gladly did. Then came the final task of lifting the trash bag into the large outdoor bin. He stood there and watched as I heaved the bag up and into the bin over his head. I looked at him. He was pretty happy and very proud of himself for helping.

That experience convicted me when I realized it was an image of my work with God. There were times when I have felt overwhelmed in ministry, as if I was pushing a boulder up a mountain or lifting a huge bag over my head. I felt ministry was a duty that I did alone. I thought ministry was about me taking out the trash for my Father. What I failed to realize is that it was an impossible task unless He was with me doing the heavy lifting. I needed to see that I am the helpless child. We participate with Jesus, the way, truth and life, who is leading the work.

For the Christian aware of God's work, one response is to not participate at all. We may think, "Isn't God doing all the work?" However, God has a role for us to play. Another inappropriate response to God's invitation is to think that taking out the trash is about us. It is selfish logic if we perceive the job as ours or that we can accomplish it ourselves. God does not need us. Pride says, "Look at me. I am saving the world!" Those who try to do ministry alone may seem noble, but it goes against God's way and is, in reality, impossible.

The world has become littered with evil, bad intentions and horrendous deeds that stink in God's world. Fortunately, God is reconciling the world to himself through Jesus (2 Corin. 5:19, Col. 1:20). Taking out "the trash" (sin) is God's work in His world because it is for His glory.

Just one person repenting and coming back to God is a miracle beyond us, not to mention redeeming every nation! This task is not too big for Him. That is why, in God's house, He does the heavy lifting. This ministry of reconciliation is something that God initiates, utilizes, fuels and empowers, not us. It is His idea, His passion and His energy that makes it happen. We participate. What is confounding and exciting is that God wants us, His children, to be with Him in the journey (2 Corin. 5:20).

Suffice it to say, we can do nothing apart from Jesus (John 15:5). If we hope to participate as joyful children, then we must begin with this perspective. We must humbly come to our knees and repent of any worldly methods and strategies, which will not bring proper glory to God. Our efforts alone are vain, fruitless and impossible. We must follow Jesus, who lovingly invites us into the role of trusting Him and bearing fruit.

Garden Principles

Jesus prepared His disciples for fruitful life and ministry. In both life and message, He was fully committed to relational and loving ministry and He wanted His disciples to follow that model (John 13:34-35, 14:15). To understand why this was so important, we need to go back to the beginning and explore God's heart and vision for fruitfulness.

In the Garden of Eden, God told Adam and Eve to be fruitful and multiply (Gen. 1:28). He wanted humanity to thrive and fulfill its purpose. That purpose, when humans obey, is to bear fruit and glorify God.

> *"Then the LORD God said, 'It is not good that the man should be alone; I will make him a helper fit for him.'"*
> *Genesis 2:18*

Adam needed a partner because fruitfulness requires relationship with other people. Man (or woman) alone could not fulfill God's vision. God created and commanded them both to be fruitful and multiply. Their fellowship was a model for fruitfulness not just physically but spiritually. Eve was someone who could minister to and be with and love Adam, and vice versa. They were a ministry team of two.

Sin, however, hindered this process by separating humanity from God's presence. Adam and Eve were exiled to live outside the garden, outside direct communion with God, and consequently, became less "fruitful." It is not hard to imagine that Adam and Eve's relationship was never the same. Adam was assigned to work the tough soil. Perhaps the dirt reminded him of where he came from and difficulty in bearing fruit without

God. Eve's fruitful multiplication was also affected by painful child birth.

When Jesus ministered on earth, He began restoring God's original fruitfulness mandate. Jesus knew that fellowship was needed to bear fruit. He pursued the lost and the broken. He came near to the hurting and protected the vulnerable. He pursued the disciples, made them a team and sent them out in teams. In other words, Jesus lived out God's relational design that was broken in the Garden of Eden.

It is not accidental that we pick up this theme of fruitfulness after Jesus washed the dirt off His disciples' feet. The disciples were "clean" in Christ (John 13:10) and He tells them, "I chose you and appointed you that you should go and bear fruit" (John 15:16). This harkened all the way back to Adam and Eve. Jesus was reversing the curse of humanity's fruitlessness. Jesus then dives deeper into the imagery of a fruitful life in John 15:1-5, explaining the necessity of connection with God.

"I am the true vine, and my Father is the vinedresser. Every branch in me that does not bear fruit he takes away, and every branch that does bear fruit he prunes, that it may bear more fruit. Already you are clean because of the word that I have spoken to you. Abide in me, and I in you. As the branch cannot bear fruit by itself, unless it abides in the vine, neither can you, unless you abide in me. I am the vine; you are the branches. Whoever abides in me and I in him, he it is that bears much fruit, for apart from me you can do nothing."

John 15:1–5

Jesus' words, "you can do nothing apart from me," are not dramatic. They lovingly shatter our human-centric worldview. They force us to abandon all ministry not a part of Jesus' vision, strategy and life. The better we grasp our limitedness, the better we understand our need to trust in the Unlimited One.

You may contend that we can breathe, walk, talk, go to

work and do many other things without Christ. Yes, we can do many things without Christ in a limited human-sense. Even more, we can build empires and nations without Christ. We can also destroy nations and the world we were meant to steward. However, Jesus is making it clear that God's work only goes forth in fruitfulness that comes through Him.

Jesus' perspective is eternal. His centering focus is glorifying God. When Jesus talks about fruit that lasts, He is speaking of thoughts, words and actions that glorify His Father. This is the fruitfulness God has always wanted for humanity. However, to produce this kind of fruit, one must depend on Christ. Only in and through Christ will proper God-glorifying fruit come and last.

For the last several years, my family has had a live Christmas tree in our house during December. Having a Christmas tree has always been a joyful tradition, filling our house with the warmth of Christmas. Last year, we even hiked through the forest to find a tree, cut it and bring it home. Even though it only lasted a few weeks, we decorated the tree with lights and ornaments.

Christmas trees inevitably die. No matter how much we water the tree, or admire it, it will die because it was cut off from its roots. Without connection to the ground, without roots in the soil providing nutrients, the tree will die. It may remain beautiful on the outside for a while, adorned with trinkets, but without its roots it is doomed for death and ultimately the trash.

Simultaneously over the past several years, California has had some of its worst wildfires in history. Wildfires raged throughout California in 2018 and 2019 consuming trees and displacing people. Yet, despite the intense devastation, many of those trees will come back and thrive again because of their roots. Wild trees and Christmas trees illustrate Jesus' point. The difference between life and death is having roots in the right place. For the Christian, the difference between fruitfulness and fruitlessness is having roots in Jesus.

God's fruitful design

Like many Americans, I am agriculturally ignorant. When I moved to East Africa, I had to learn quickly. Other expatriate families lived in gated compounds with elaborate and beautiful outdoor spaces, full of plants, flowers and grass. The house my wife and I moved into was bare so we thought we would try our hand at gardening. It was not easy. Some plants died, some grew too much, others barely made it. Desire alone is not good enough. For each plant, you need to know their needs, climate, time to plant and so on.

If we are called to bear fruit, then we need an expert Gardener. We will not be fruitful on our own. We need the tender care of the One who knows our needs and we need our Savior who provides us with life-giving nutrients. We need this both for ourselves and those around us.

Jesus had no intention of letting His followers wither and die spiritually after He left and returned to the Father. In fact, He told them, "I will not leave you as orphans … Because I live, you also will live" (John 14:18a, 19b). Jesus wanted His disciples to live and bear fruit through His life in them.

This imagery of a fruitful life would not have been new for the Jewish disciples. The prophet Isaiah called Israel the "vineyard of the Lord" (Isa. 5:7). King David said, "The righteous flourish like the palm tree … they still bear fruit in old age" (Ps. 92:12-14). From Adam to Jesus, God wanted a righteous people, connected with Him, who would bear fruit even in a broken world. What Jesus revealed is that He is the source of life.

God wants fruit while the world wants ornaments. The world is more concerned with outward success and temporary beauty. However, ornaments (trinkets on Christmas trees) do not fool the true Gardener or impress Him. Dying trees only look good for a time. Ornaments can even look like fruit for the undiscerning, but time is the ultimate indicator of authenticity. When the ornaments fade and nothing sprouts from within, a tree is seen for its true colors, judged by its lack of roots.

Without roots, the tree is destined to be futile, frail and fatal. Jesus says, "If anyone does not abide in me he is thrown away like a branch and withers; and the branches are gathered, thrown into the fire, and burned" (John 15:6). That is exactly what happens to my Christmas tree every January.

God wants life to grow and multiply because He is the living God. Nature teaches us that life breeds life. God built multiplication into the DNA of nature because it expands the living world. It is a brilliant way for life to flourish and expand. Look around at nature: the grass, birds, trees and ants that invade our kitchens. Life brings multiplication and reproduction. Psalm 19 says that creation shows us the glory of God. He created what we see to reveal Himself, so growth and multiplication specifically reveal something about God.

Paul reiterates this idea in Romans when he says that God's divine nature is revealed in physical nature. The created world shows us several attributes like God's power, creativity, brilliance and love. Like an artist expressing themselves in a painting, God's identity is seen in His creative actions. By staring at a Van Gogh, one can understand a little bit about his life, both his internal life and the way he perceived the world. The physical world and creation are a spectacular living canvas that puts the living God on display.

Being in nature is life-giving for me. I feel small and insignificant amidst jagged mountains, raging rivers and towering trees that do not require my presence for their existence. Yet, ironically, in those situations where I feel most out of control, I feel most alive. Nature takes attention off ourselves. It forces us to realize our neediness, dependence and relative insignificance surrounded by creations of a powerful Creator. When the attention is off of ourselves, we properly interact with the universe in awe, wonder and humble appreciation. This kind of perspective actually brings a refreshing release of burdens and stress if we simultaneously understand that there is a wonderful Provider who cares for us.

Some of my most vivid times with God have been in nature,

beside a quiet lake in the cool morning or on top of a mountain being touched by the rays of sun as it rises over the horizon. In nature, spiritual truths come alive. God made us to see His provision in the rain and faithfulness in the constant sunrise. These experiences go beyond my natural senses. When I am overtaken by beauty, I actually become more aware of the Creator of beauty. I see God's beautiful design, heart and desire to provide. He earns our trust when we pay attention to nature.

Nature is meant to be a part of the human experience. It is one of God's greatest teachers, reminding humanity about fruitfulness and God's principles for multiplication. Sometimes God uses nature to shape His people. Nature takes attention off of ourselves and forces us to realize our dependence upon God. The barren wilderness can even be an accelerator for people to grow with God by learning to trust. Moses's and Israel's character were built in the desert and they learned to see God as Provider. King David learned his craft of shepherding in the wilderness and knew the Messiah would be a Great Shepherd. Jesus was tested in the wilderness and chose to retreat to quiet places to commune with the Father. Thus, nature's design and qualities make it uniquely suited to increase faith when that trust is properly put in the Provider.

One of God's magnificent natural processes is bearing fruit. Fruit, in the general sense, demonstrates two things in the life-growing process. First, fruit reveals identity. When something bears fruit, it signifies the health of a living thing. Dead plants do not bear fruit. Only living things create fruit. Second, fruit causes increase. Fruit is essentially the spawning of one thing into more.

God's command to humanity to be "fruitful and multiply" was as natural as an apple tree. Since life puts the living God on display, it makes sense that the multiplication of life would bring glory to God. God's plan is not complicated, but it is dependent on Him.

Interestingly, the command to multiply (Gen. 1:28) comes right after the proclamation of our identity, being made in the image of God (Gen. 1:27). God did not just give us dominion, but stewardship as His image. Humans, being in His image, are apex glory-bearers on earth made to rule over that which God created. Our image and identity are meant to inspire increase because it is about the One whom we bear the image of.

We should pause and consider the spiritual war that was waged by Satan in the garden against God and humanity. Satan hates our identity and he hates the dominion we are given. He hates when we are fruitful and multiply. That is why Satan wants sin, which leads to death. Death is the opposite of life, fruit and multiplication. Death stops the intended process of growth and multiplication. Only in Jesus can we recover God's intended design for humanity.

Roots of trust in Jesus

There is an important connection between trust and fruitfulness. Fruitfulness requires trust, which is why the disciples needed to walk in trust with God and Jesus in order to bear the fruit of love. Jesus said, "Trust in God. Trust also in me" (John 14:1 NLT). Trust is a relational term and the disciples, and us, need to be relationally restored to God to be fruitful gardeners.

Interestingly, both Judas and Peter would demonstrate a lack of trust. Jesus predicted Judas's betrayal: the ultimate failure of trust in Jesus, rejecting His identity and relationship (John 13:21-30). Jesus also told Peter that he would deny Him (John 13:36-38). While both men failed to trust in Jesus, it seems that only Peter's trust and relationship was restored.

Trust in God could not be more essential and foundational in Jesus' plan to reach the world. Trust binds two parties. It binds disciples to Jesus and His plans. When we connect to Jesus the Vine in trust, we live, grow and labor with Him. Jesus asked His disciples to trust in Him because, spiritually speaking, what we trust in is where we put our roots. Trust is foundational to our worldview, providing a base for our spiritual life. It is what we connect to and live out of. We are hard-wired to trust in something and we were intended to trust in God.

In a world with billions of options and opportunities, we need to trust in something. We are finite and confined. Eventually, we will spiritually place our stakes in something we hope and trust in. This is true for everyone. What makes Christ-followers different is where we put our roots.

God made us, intended for us, to place our roots in Him because He is Creator and Sustainer. We were meant to believe that God is our Provider and act on it. When we do so, we can properly relate to God and His creation. As Dave Benson, director of the centre for culture and discipleship with The London Institute for Contemporary Christianity, says, "We care for the garden, God cares for us."

If the word "trust" is too vague, think of the practical term "reliance." Everyone relies on something. Everyone picks something in our vast world to make a firm foundation. What you rely on is that which you consistently go to in order to feel alive, get by and reset. It may be many things for different times and seasons or it may be one consistent thing like a person, place or passion.

Why would we put roots in something not infinite and eternal? Anything less than the perfect Provider is offensive to Him and detrimental to us. God wants to be the place where we find stability, not because He is greedy but because He is the best choice and the only One who can handle such a task.

In love, God gives people freedom to choose what they will tether their lives to. Tethering our soul to a foundation is an act of trust. It is the most basic form of trust, like infants building bonds with a mother and father. Since we are not the originators of life, we must get life from somewhere. Choosing wrongly means losing life. Choosing Him means growth and reproduction. That is why Jesus boldly said that His disciples' roots must be firmly connected to Him. Jesus gives His disciples a reason they can trust in Him. He says, "In my Father's house are many rooms. If it were not so, would I have told you that I go to prepare a place for you? And if I go and prepare a place for you, I will come again and will take you to myself, that where I am you may be also" (John 14:2-3).

Trusting in Jesus is worth it. Our eternal hope is an eternal home with an eternal family. How I wish Jesus would have given us more details about the Father's house and what awaits the faithful! Still, as short as they are, these sentences provide more hope than most anything else on earth. One day, we will know our trust is well founded. The interesting connection about our future home is that we must dwell in Him now to get there. Jesus calls this abiding and we will look at this more later.

If trust in God is where we put our roots, then truth is the nutrition we need. When we trust in Christ, who Himself is the truth, we live, grow and bear fruit. Trust deepens relationships. The more we know and trust Jesus, the more our relationship with Him will grow and the more fruit we will produce.

Making disciples is spiritual gardening

Jesus' plan is for His disciples to multiply fruitfulness. He left for this reason and He is still working for this purpose. The mission is still His and our small role is to faithfully bear His fruit in our lives and others.

Jesus told a parable about a master who left his vineyard to tenants. The tenants were tasked to grow and multiply what was left to them. Instead of being faithful, they rebelled. This was Israel's failure to cultivate fruit in the nations. Jesus said, "Therefore I tell you, the kingdom of God will be taken away from you and given to a people producing its fruits." (Matt. 21:43).

> *"By this my Father is glorified, that you bear much fruit and so prove to be my disciples."*

Disciples bear fruit for God's glory. When we bear fruit, we recover our role as fruitful co-laborers in the garden. Our role, however, goes beyond ourselves. Jesus wanted His disciples to help others bear fruit as well. Disciple making, then, is helping others be fruitful. We do this through helping shape people's trust in God. The greater the trust, the greater the intimacy with God and the greater the fruitfulness.

Of course, we cannot do this alone. We have the Holy Spirit leading and guiding. We participate by using the tools He gives. Two of our greatest gardening tools are the Scriptures (God's words to us) and prayer (talking to God). It is essential to realize that these are relational tools because union with God is a relational process. That is why our mandate of disciple-making is a relational venture, not a religious one.

Disciples know the truth and share the truth. They know truth in relationship with God and they share truth in relationship with others. Disciples know that God's Word accomplishes His work. Therefore, we step into His work when we obey His words. Obeying is joining what He has already planned and spoken.

Gardening is hard work but prayer with the Father, the Gardener, makes our work collaborative and possible. In our limitedness, our prayers show that we cannot accomplish the supernatural work of God alone. Yet, in God's wonderful invitation and commissioning, our prayers propel us far beyond our inability. In the smallest way, our asking ushers in His powerful work through us.

Fruitful Abiding

"I will not leave you as orphans."
John 14:18a

Several years ago, I had dinner with a pastor who had been in jail in Asia, accused of sharing his faith. His time in jail was in a crowded cell. Only a few people could lay down at a time because the cell was overcrowded. The others would stand and give room for those resting. Inside the room was one open toilet to share.

As I listened, the thought of such a difficult condition made me uneasy. Yet, when I asked him about it, he was filled with joy. "It was wonderful," he essentially said with a smile. "Everyone had to listen to me talk about Jesus!" As you can imagine, his response shocked and challenged me. His story is a testimony to the power and joy of Jesus' abiding presence. Jesus has not left us alone. He is with us in castles, cathedrals and concrete cells. He is near for our sake and for the sake of the mission He has entrusted us with. And, like my pastor friend, His presence becomes more valuable the more difficult the mission becomes.

Jesus assured the disciples of His presence because of what lay ahead. However, instead of walking with Jesus physically, the disciples would need to learn to abide. John 15:5 makes it clear that Jesus' presence was just as important for the disciples after He returned to the Father. Jesus said, "Whoever abides in me and I in him, he it is that bears much fruit, for apart from me you can do nothing." It seems that, for us and the disciples, abiding in Christ is the only way we will accomplish God's mission of bearing fruit.

Mutual abiding

Abiding must be learned. It requires sight of the unseen and knowledge of the reality that God is near. Fortunately, Jesus' garden analogy in John 15 helps paint a practical picture of what abiding looks like.

One of the key truths of abiding is that it is a symbiotic relationship. In Christ, the Vine, we receive life, nourishment and shade. Through Him, we bear precious fruit that brings honor to Him and fruit for the Gardener. The Gardener, in turn, watches over the entire process and provides protection.

We can understand mutual abiding by considering the relationship between New York City and the United States. New York City is in the United States and the United States is in New York City. America includes New York City and New York City is American. Though they are separate, and one is greater in size and authority, they are both simultaneously in one another. This would not be true for independent and separate entities like the United States and Canada.

Like a country, we pledge our allegiance to that which we abide in. It changes our "citizenship" and we receive the rights and inheritance of that kingdom. So, abiding in Christ unites us in common identity, purpose and benefits and our civic duty is lived out in loving trust.

The uncomfortable adjustment is that we must come under Christ's authority. Our old nature wrestles with authority, but Christ lovingly sets us free from the burden of judgement and being the judge. God's authority does not diminish our relationship with Him; it enhances it. It is loving, not oppressive. Jesus' authority actually frees us from the compulsion of our old nature. We no longer need to be the moral authority. Instead, we get to freely live in joyful obedience.

Us in God

Besides seeing family, one of my favorite activities when visiting the United Kingdom is to walk around castles and old ruins. These majestic structures are an image of power and safety. Though most people see them just as fortresses, they were also homes to dwell in. Castles were sturdy defenses from the enemy on the outside and ornate, beautiful residences on the inside.

Our modern word for abode, a home, comes from the same origin as "abide" and the castle imagery illustrates the dichotomy of both protection on the outside and life-giving relationship on the inside. Abiding in Christ provides refuge and safety, as well as beauty and rest.

We can rest safely in Christ because we trust in Him. It is about God's work, not ours. We do not build a castle to live in. We come into His protection and intimacy at His invitation. This protection does not give us license to be absent and avoid the world. It is quite the opposite. It protects us in order to prepare us for missional engagement in the world.

God in us

As my imprisoned friend demonstrated, abiding has nothing to do with where we are and everything to do with who we are with. Abiding is a beautiful relational term that implies God is with us and in us. The Spirit of God dwells in us and provides the power for obedience, mission and bearing fruit. If God is in us, then abiding is not a place where we charge our battery and go out in the world. It is something that is always with us to empower every good work.

I was discussing ministry with a friend at my church and he said, "I am just not qualified to do ministry right now." He did not feel "good enough." His comment portrayed a feeling that many Christians have. Yes, we are unqualified in our flesh and must actively fight our fleshly desires and bring them to the light. And, there are qualifications and indicators for leadership in the church, and organizations may have requirements. However, we must also remember that God calls and qualifies His saints, not us. When we participate with God in His mission on earth, we need no further badge or approval.

No one is good but God (Mark 10:18). There is no human good enough for God's mission except Christ, which is why Jesus abides in every believer, empowers us and will never fail us (Gal. 2:20, Col. 1:27). There is only one qualification to partner with God in ministry: Christ in us. In Him, we have full access to God.

If we disqualify ourselves from laboring with God, we are claiming that Christ in us is not good enough. When we act this way, it reduces ministry to a religious striving that contradicts the Gospel. It makes the Gospel more about us becoming better people than participating with God to make Him known. We need to realize that broken vessels do not limit God's work. If anything, they shine Him brighter.

Actively abiding

The dichotomy of us in God and Him in us creates a unique tension. On one hand, we are free from the burden to accomplish God's work because He works in and through us. On the other hand, we are not exempt from actively participating. The implication is both trust and passion, faith and mission, spiritual rest and physical action.

This begins with resting in God. We must trust God's work, for there is no eternal work that is not empowered by Him. Nana Yaw, global associate director for generations for The Lausanne Movement, says, "John 15 circles around the theme of patience, abiding patiently with calm assurance of both faith and hope that the Father's love cares diligently for every branch in the vine. This is a value that seems to be getting lost in today's nano generation. Waiting is easily perceived as wasting, and often we rush ahead of God."[3] When we try to rush ahead of God, we attempt the impossible. On the other hand, we do have a role to play and we must be careful not to stifle the work of God in and through us.

Proper abiding should also lead to work, for God is working. Abiding is not a place where we begin our own work. It is the place where God does His work in and through us.

When I was in college, I worked at an outdoor camp. I was tasked with helping lead the high ropes course, which is a set of obstacles about 10-20 feet off the ground and required campers to put on a harness and helmet and walk through the obstacles. At the end of the course was a zip line that glided the campers down to the ground.

When we prepared the campers, we would explain how sturdy the equipment was. For example, the lines holding them could withstand the weight of an entire car. It was more than safe for one person. So, when I asked, "How many of you trust this course?" Just about all the campers raised their hands. However, when I asked, "Now, how many of you want to go up on the ropes course?" only a few raised their hands.

They knew it was safe, but wouldn't walk on it. This is the disconnect with many of us. Our cerebral understanding is there. We say we trust God. We know He should be safe, but we will not take the first step in obedience. When we fail to act, our trust is inactive and our faith proven invalid, refusing to follow the Way, Truth and Life. The apostle John says, "Whoever says he abides in Him ought to walk in the same way in which he walked." (1 John 2:6). To abide is to walk out our faith in Jesus in obedience, proving Him to be good and safe. There can be no proper abiding without missional obedience.

Since Jesus is actively moving, then we must actively follow and it is through our courageous following on the high ropes that brings attention to our Leader. If our abiding does not result in practical and physical obedience, then our trust is simply a fascination; it is not faith. We cannot take the sweet abiding and forego the risky assignments. Abiding is not just about resting by a fireplace; it is also about walking through the fire in obedience.

The Spirit in us is more than sufficient for the task at hand. God's work should not overwhelm us. His burden is light and He loving leads us, providing all we need to obey. The courage we require comes from a change in perspective that God is with us. God's presence overcomes any fear we may have. Jesus is with us on the high ropes. He has gone before us and He has led many safely through.

The fruit of abiding

"If you abide in me, and my words abide in you, ask whatever you wish, and it will be done for you. By this my Father is glorified, that you bear much fruit and so prove to be my disciples."

John 15:7-8

I grew up picking fruit with my family at farms. Depending on the season, my mother would take us to apple orchards, pumpkin patches and berry farms. It does not take an expert to know good fruit, which is why some of the best fruit never made it made it into my bucket!

Jesus said that people are known by their good or bad fruit (Matt. 7:16-20). His point is not that some fruit is hard to see or that the good and bad are hard to discern. He did not say that godly fruit is visible and worldly fruit is invisible. Both are visible and people can naturally discern the good and bad. The principle is that what people exhibit on the outside is a testimony about what is on the inside.

Only those in Christ can exhibit God's fruit. The apostle Paul said the fruit of the Spirit is love, joy, peace, patience, kindness, goodness, faithfulness, gentleness and self-control (Gal. 5:22-23). Paul's point is that the Spirit manifests these in us and through us. Paul's use of the singular form of "fruit" seems to suggest that we should view this as one fruit from the

Spirit instead of many (Keller, Galatians for You), like a fruit with many flavors. What is clear is that the Spirit's fruit is not naturally found in us or the world, so when the world sees godly fruit it is clear that God is involved.

I want to unpack three aspects of the fruit that we bear when we abide in Jesus.

1. Fruit is for the Father's glory. Just as an apple is not for the apple tree, the fruit is not for the fruit-bearer. Jesus is bearing fruit for the sake of others and God's glory. Like a novice hiker trying to climb Mount Everest, we need Jesus' in us because we cannot glorify the Father on our own. We need His words because His words are His will. We need to faithfully obey His will and path because only His way can put God on display.

If God is the source of our fruit, then fruit is anything that comes from God and imitates God. Fruit is the manifestation of God's likeness. We were made in God's image so we could glorify Him by manifesting godly fruit. This godly fruit brings God glory. Where there is godly fruit, God's likeness is expanded and shown; it is put on display. This explains why bearing fruit must be a relational process with God. Only His efforts will result in His glory.

I failed to understand this concept early in my faith. I thought that fruit was an external badge that God gives to successful Christians. Fruit was a status for my honor. I wanted to be a fruitful tree, but my faith was more about worldly ornaments than faithful fruit. Essentially, I wanted God's blessing for my acts of 'goodness' instead of asking God to pour His goodness through me. I thought I had goodness to offer the world and I wanted people to see my goodness, not His in me. It was a religiously-disguised striving. In reality, all such efforts are impossible, a never-satisfying road that leads to doubt, burnout, apostasy, or depression.

This was the challenge of the Pharisees, who failed to bear real fruit. They did not glorify God because they refused to listen to Jesus (John 5:39). They wanted an image of righteousness but could not humble themselves to be reborn. They wanted the glory instead of letting God's glory work through them.

Our asking is an important part of the journey. By asking us to ask, Jesus is inviting us to participate. This invitation is proof of His desire for partnership. He wants to be with us along the way. He already knows what we will ask before we do, so asking His words provides us a practical way to participate. And, we must ask His words or we will wander from His authority. He knows we don't know everything so He invites us to participate through prayer, divine wondering, not wandering.

When we ask, we demonstrate a spirit of willingness to participate like a son joyfully joining his father. Asking honors God's ability to answer and shows a submission to His authority. We can trust that He will say "yes" or "no" based on His will, not ours.

Since He has already initiated the process through His words in us, our asking according to His word takes root in a firm foundation that will be fruitful. Jesus' words bring authority and align us with the Father's heart. His words focus our efforts on His glory, not our own.

Our asking does not cheapen the relationship, it strengthens it. It dignifies us and honors Him. Asking shows that we understand His purpose, we agree with it and trust Him to act. He may even wait for us to ask so that we have the privilege of participation.

2. Fruit is evangelistic. Good fruit tastes good and nothing tastes better than God's love. This is why Jesus wanted His disciples to be known for their love (John 13:35). Jesus wanted His love to be seen in His disciples and reveal a loving God to the world.

This kind of "lay down your life for another" love is evangelistic. It is so foreign that it causes people to stop and wonder, where could this love come from? This is the kind of love that forgives the most grievous crime. It is a love that adopts the unlovable, stands up for the most hated and dies for the hater. Any action of love we take will naturally mimic what Christ has already done for us. This kind of love takes a big spotlight and points to heaven. It also shows we are in communion with this wonderful God and identifies us as legitimate children of God.

We are vessels that not only glorify God, but also, through our actions, testify to God before the world. Fruit helps the world to taste and see God. That is why godly fruit cannot be just a feeling or idea; it must be something that reveals God. Fruit demonstrates God's incredible nature and goodness to a skeptical and hateful world. A person could stand on the roadside and shout "I love you!" to strangers all day, but no one would consider that person loving. However, if that person rushed in front of a vehicle to save a wandering child, people would proclaim, "What love!"

3. Fruit is for fellowship. Fruit is manifest in situations and relationships. This may seem obvious, but Jesus commands His disciples to love one another. There is a recipient of God's love. It is for other people.

God's love meets needs. In blessing others in practical and tangible ways, fruit strengthens, redeems and restores broken relationships. Fruit has a strategic and practical role in mending relationships on earth. When we are loving, joyful, patient and kind, relationships get stronger.

Take John 3:16 for example. It says that because God loved the world, He gave His son so that those who believe can be saved. Jesus demonstrated and revealed God's love for us. The need was salvation. The motivation was compassionate love. The expression was giving something valuable, revealing God's love and salvation. The result was access to fellowship with God.

If God is in us, He will lead us to love those around us, manifesting the characteristic of His Spirit. We often think of love as a warm feeling but the Bible refers to *agape* (love) more in sense of charity. When Paul speaks of love as fruit, he means an affectionate action expressed towards someone. God's love through us is often practical and visible. It is an action between a lover and a beloved that results in a greater relationship.

Practically speaking, it means that when relationships are breaking, God can reveal His faithfulness though us. When people have tangible needs, we meet those needs in love. When the world is harsh, we can show God's gentleness. In this way, God's love in us actually binds relationships.

SECTION 2

Friendship on Mission:
The Path of Jesus

Joining Your Story to God's Glory

*"You are my friends if you do what I command you. No longer
do I call you servants, for the servant does not know what
his master is doing; but I have called you friends, for all that
I have heard from my Father I have made known to you."*
John 15:14-15

Jesus' words In John 15 are shocking. The Creator of the
universe had already come to earth and would soon die to save
His creation. Then, He went even further to close the relational
gap and called His followers friends.

When it comes to Jesus and His disciples, it is hard to
separate His mission from their friendship. The disciples
were Jesus' friends and knew "what the master is doing." One
translation says, "the master's business."[4] For the disciples,
joining Jesus in the Master's work was a fundamental part of
their friendship with Him.

Like a friend sharing deep and personal information, the
fact that Jesus shared the Father's plan honored the disciples.
More than that, sharing the Father's business was an invitation
into the work as co-laborers. The Father shared His plans with
Jesus and Jesus shared with His disciples.

Our friendship with Christ is not a lighthearted matter.
We need to take it seriously. We need to take it seriously and
understand the weight of it so we can faithfully follow. Like an
apprentice, we must learn the Master's business to co-labor
effectively.

*"I glorified you on earth, having accomplished the
work that you gave me to do. And now, Father,*

glorify me in your own presence with the glory
that I had with you before the world existed."
John 17:4-5

"All mine are yours, and yours are mine,
and I am glorified in them."
John 17:10

At the heart of our mission with Christ is God's desire to be known, seen and glorified. One cannot emphasize this enough. It must be done God's way and the implication of this text is that God is glorified when He is relationally known. There cannot be glorification if no one beholds it. Relationship, then, is a foundation through which God reveals Himself. That is why Jesus wanted to be glorified in the presence of the Father and Jesus was glorified in relationship with His disciples.

Part of our mission as friends of God is to know Him. If relationship with God is a tool to reveal God, then a deeper relationship will provide greater glorification. In being invited into closer proximity through friendship, we are able to reveal Him more.

We are intimately called into a grand narrative far beyond our understanding. We are called up on stage not just to get a closer look but also to join in. Jesus, the main actor in this narrative, is at the center. Christ takes the spotlight by perfectly, "accomplishing the work" God gave Him. Yet, the story does not stop with Jesus glorifying God. Jesus' followers and friends are called into the rest of the story, taking the stage because Jesus can be glorified through us.

God's story is about God's glory. We are not called to be on stage to take the spotlight, but to provide the spotlight. If we are friend with Jesus then we must humbly step on stage for His glory, not our own.

This friendship, a mutual bonding for the benefit of the other, ties us to God's story. It links us to the plot. It is not just good for God; it is also beneficial for us. In the narrative, it is the same cross that revealed God's glory and saved humanity. In the cross, we see a magnificent display and example that what is good for God is good for us. Relationship with God links us to Him and makes us an avenue for His glorification. That is why Paul was able to say that that God is working all things for the good of those who love God (Rom. 8:28). For friends of God, there is no dichotomy between our good and God's glory.

A passion for God's presence

God chose Moses for a special task and spoke to him like a friend. Moses, a human with failures just like us, was able to enter into a special relationship with Yahweh (the personal name for God in the Old Testament). Moses played his part well because he knew what we must know: God deserves to be glorified and He made humans to do this.

We see this story in the book of Exodus. Israel angered God in the wilderness so God said He would not go with them. Instead, He would send Israel on ahead without Him to the Promised Land. However, Moses knew God's heart.

Moses knew that Israel needed God's presence for the mission and that God's relational presence with Israel would bring God glory. Moses pleaded with God, "… 'If your presence will not go with me, do not bring us up from here. For how shall it be known that I have found favor in your sight, I and your people? Is it not in your going with us, so that we are distinct, I and your people, from every other people on the face of the earth?'" (Exod. 33:15b-16)? Moses was passionate about the presence of God. He knew that if God is not involved in the mission then Israel's activity would be carried out in vain.

We need God's presence to participate in His mission and this should drive us into a passionate pursuit of God's presence. Like a good friend, this pursuit is more than just knowing about Yahweh. It is about a loving, intimate and obedient relationship with God that puts Him on display before the lost world.

Our relationship with God carries the same opportunity that

Moses had because our core mission is the same: to reveal the glory of God. Because something cannot be revealed if it is not present, God's presence must be at the center of our lives and activity. We must cease all efforts where God's presence and glory is not the aim. We should repent of any human-centric initiatives that foolishly try to accomplish God's mission on earth without Him. Christ is the main actor. Our efforts alone will only glorify ourselves. Our only option, like Moses, is to boldly ask God to reveal His presence through us.

When God invites us into relationship, it matters how we respond. We can learn from Moses what it means to be a good friend. As friends and followers, we cry for intimacy, come in humility and respond in worshipful obedience

Intimacy

When we interact with the living God, we should cry out for intimacy with Him. The world ignores, downplays and lies about the glory of God. Satan wants the world to doubt God's existence and goodness. The apostle Paul says, "In their case the god of this world has blinded the minds of the unbelievers, to keep them from seeing the light of the gospel of the glory of Christ, who is the image of God" (2 Cor. 4:4). We, however, who have tasted His goodness, will respond like Moses in eager expectation of a deeper relationship.

You may think that Moses's bold request for God's presence would have been enough. I myself would have likely stopped after that. Instead, Moses declares, "Now show me your glory" (Exod. 33:18 NIV). For a man with a stuttering tongue, he was a bold man! Moses already had assurance of the mission, but he wanted more. He wanted what we truly long for: to intimately know God's glory. Moses essentially said, "Show me what it is all about. I want to see your fullness, everything I am living for! I want to fully know who you are" Moses was not asking for miracles. He wanted to know the Source of the miracles. He wanted to see God's fullness.

Moses honored God with a plea for intimacy. In that moment, Moses was not trying earn God's favor. He was crying out for a greater depth of understanding of his God. Moses knew his relationship with God was not just a disposable tool for God's mission. The mission and our relationship to the Author go hand in hand. Moses did not just want God to be revealed in the mission, Moses wanted to deeply know the God he was walking with. Our requests to know God honor Him. That is why God was willing to oblige Moses's request and reveal Himself (as much as possible).

For those who struggle to interact with God on a personal level, we may wonder how we could we ever fully know God. Are not we just mere humans? This self-doubting is counterproductive. He has already invited into relationship for His praise. Though God's wonder and glory is magnificent, it is hidden and revealed at His discretion. God's is not reckless in revealing His glory and He has favorably chosen people to be the precious bearers and observers of His glory.

There is no doubt God wants us to know His glory to increase our intimacy. Jesus prayed, "Father, I desire that they also, whom you have given me, may be with me where I am, to see my glory that you have given me because you loved me before the foundation of the world" (John 17:24). The passion for our intimacy comes from knowing that God Himself is our great reward and one day we will receive the intimacy we desire.

Humility

God's glory and presence comes with an unimaginable power. There is no hindrance to the force of His work. Thus, He is always before us in plans and His work precedes us because He is more loving, good and powerful than us. He will accomplish what He wants. What this means is that we cannot love our lost neighbor more than God. We cannot care for the suffering more than God.

The only proper response is humble acceptance of His will

and power. He knows the best way to be glorified and He will accomplish His plans. Followers who want the same thing know they must depend on His presence.

Humility is the posture that allows God to shine brighter in us and this humility comes naturally when we stand in awe of His significance and capability.

Those who are closest to God depend on Him the most. Moses' heart of dependence grew through his experiences with God. Moses saw God deliver His people out of slavery in Egypt through the mighty plagues. Moses endured Pharaoh's criticisms and oppression as He represented God in Egypt. Moses crossed the dry Red Sea with God's people. It would have been utter insanity for Moses to take credit for the miracles God did through him. Moses knew that his participation was not for personal comfort and gain. The plagues in Egypt and the opening of the Red Sea were not for Moses's enjoyment, fulfillment or calling. The miracles were for God's glory in His story, revealing Himself to the world.

To participate well, we need hearts of trust. As Moses showed, trusting humility is not without confidence. We need not be timid. We are known and redeemed to make Him known and renown. God was willing to oblige Moses's request because Moses appealed to God's ultimate mission, the revealing of His glory. The Lord responded to Moses, "'This very thing that you have spoken I will do, for you have found favor in my sight, and I know you by name'" (Exod. 33:17b). God was pleased because His plan is to accompany His people. So, we follow Moses' example when we humbly pray for God's glory to be revealed in the world.

Worshipful obedience

It has been said that, "God is most glorified in us when we are most satisfied in Him."[5] This is true, but we must also consider the coinciding principle: we are most satisfied when God is most glorified. We must take the perspective off of ourselves, our efforts and our initiative. Our deepest desire is to be behold. We wait on His revelation because He initiatives the process of revealing Himself. As worshippers, when we make God's magnificent glory central, and stand in awe of it, we are then satisfied.

If God is perfectly content, loving and powerful, why does He want to reveal Himself? Some may think that God's desire for glory and worship is vain, but there are two reasons against that logic. First, God deserves it. He is not conjuring false worship. Our worship is not forced. It is recognition of the facts; the way things are. We were meant to worship Him in freedom. We choose what we worship. He is not intimidated by our free will because He knows the value of His own glory.

Jesus deserves the glory because He had it before time began and because He rightly glorified the Father by doing God's work on earth. Jesus said, "... 'Father, the hour has come; glorify your Son that the Son may glorify you ... I glorified you on earth, having accomplished the work that you gave me to do. And now, Father, glorify me in your own presence with the glory that I had with you before the world existed'" (John 17:1b, 4-5). Jesus' glory pre-existed us and the universe. Thus, He deserves praise and can perfectly steward our worship without vanity.

The second reason God's desire for glory is not vain is because we were made to glorify Him. God's glory reveals His worth and value, which is infinite. Everything comes from Him so everything finds its purpose and meaning in Him, in relationship to the Creator. Since we are His creation, when He is glorified, we are dignified. God's revelation lovingly affirms human existence, identity and purpose.

People are hard-wired to respond in worship to that which we find beautiful and valuable. We were made from Him and through Him. He is the source of our being, existence and purpose. So, it makes sense that we fit properly in alignment with Him and the created order of the universe most when we praise Him. It is not to our detriment when we worship, it is for our joy and blessing. We love worship because we were made for it and it is good for us.

As to why God reveals His glory, the answer, then, is that God reveals Himself for His pleasure and our benefit. He can bless us because His glory is not dependent on us. Dependent glory would not perfectly glorious; it would be a diminishing or variant glory. That is why God will not share his glory with another (Is. 42:8).

Our gazing at the glory does not add to its beauty no more than gazing at diamond increases its value. God's glory does not fluctuate and that is good so that it can truly bless the beholder. That more valuable that which is seen and beheld, the better it is for the beholder resulting in greater worship.

When the Word became flesh, it allowed humanity to see the glory of God in a new way, in the person of Jesus (John 1:14). Jesus came for us, not that we would be additional worshippers in an empty choir but that we would be saved. His mission was a rescue mission, not just to save us from Hell, but to save us for worship. Worship is a blessing we get like the angels in heaven who joyfully and voluntarily praise God endlessly. We get the same privilege as we grow in friendship with God, we see His glory more, resulting in greater worship in the magnitude it is revealed.

Pursuing People

*"This is my commandment, that you love
one another as I have loved you."*
John 15:12

Jesus commanded His disciples to love because God is glorified when we love like Him. Though it is not easy, the call is clear. We must learn to love people like Jesus and to learn this kind of love we must experience it firsthand.

Though we may not meet Christ personally, we experience His pursuit through His Spirit, His Word, His creation and His saints. Through these, we become aware of God's powerful work on our behalf which changes us, awakens us and leads us into deeper relationship. This awareness and conviction anchors us in a passionate pursuit for others.

Many years ago, I was at a personal crossroads. I was wrestling with questions about my future and decisions I needed to make as a young man. The weight of the decisions was overwhelming. I needed to hear from God so I packed a small bag and started walking towards the nearest forest. I walked until I found a fallen tree. I climbed up it and sat quietly. It was there that I opened the Scriptures.

When I sat down, the Spirit led me to one Bible verse. Instantly, my soul was filled with peace. Though the verse did not give me specific answers to my decisions, it gave me something better: awareness of God's presence and love for me. It was as if He was there and knew exactly what I needed to hear. That moment shifted the perspective of my soul. I was not alone. My Savior had heard every anxious prayer and doubt. It is hard to describe the energy and joy that filled my soul as I practically ran back home through the forest!

The art of fishing

Jesus ministry strategy was simple, revolutionary and world-changing. It is not a coincidence that there has never been a more people-focused leader than Jesus and there will never be anyone as successful as Jesus in ministry. Jesus changed the world with the way He pursued people with passion, strategy and success.

Recently, I was able to go fly fishing, which is a serious hobby in my state. A fly fisherman's dedication is, quite frankly, admirable. They will often get up early, travel for miles, and then wait for hours for the chance to catch one fish. While I do not share that same level of passion, I learned to appreciate their determination and commitment. I learned that fishing requires intimate knowledge of the fish they want to catch. It requires skill as well as patience. A good fisher knows what the fish eat, when they eat and where they eat. This is not much different from our call to make disciples.

If we want to love people like Jesus, we need to fish like Him. Jesus' had an incredible passion for people, but He also knew who, how and where to "catch" people. If there was any secret to His ministry, it is that Jesus won people with love. He fished with love. His love changed people, shaped people, and rarely did anyone remain the same. This kind of love is contagious. When we love people like Jesus, more people will love like Him.

Jesus told Peter and Andrew, "Follow me and I will make you fishers of men" (Matt. 4:19b). There is both friendship and mission in this statement. Jesus is asking Peter and Andrew to follow Him, to know Him and His ways, in relationship with Him. Along the way, they were changed by being around Him. Their relationship was never just about the three of them. To be with Jesus and like Jesus, is to be outwardly focused like Jesus.

Jesus invited people to learn and grow and always go deeper in relationship. For this reason, the disciples, as imperfect as they were, made better vessels to change the world than the Pharisees. The disciples knew they were not caught for their inherent goodness. They were caught because God's love is unexplainable and overflowing.

> *"By this all people will know that you are my*
> *disciples, if you have love for one another."*
> *John 13:35*

How we love matters because it reveals who God is and whether we follow Him. God's love is uniquely identifiably. It is unconditional and purposeful, faithful and hopeful, relationally motivated and missionally productive. Jesus never gives up on people, because His love is for them despite their condition. People like the rich young ruler may walk away from Jesus, but He will never walk away from people. In fact, it is people's lost-ness that makes Jesus pursue them.

Though we pursue in love, not all will respond in love. God's love is kind, but it also confronts and challenges. Fishing requires tact, wisdom and patience. It is an uncomfortable process, sometimes awkward, sometimes dangerous. The world is not used to the kind of intentionality that Jesus puts in our hearts.

Despite opposition, godly love pursues for the good of the pursued and the health of the relationship. We see this first in the Garden when sin enters and God goes "looking" for Adam and Eve because division was created. Sin hinders relationships, but love restores and binds. This is why God's quest is to restore relational intimacy first with Him and then with others.

God's fishing strategy reflects His heart and nature. Christ's work was to make the Father known in order that people may have eternal life in God (John 17:3-4). So eternal life is first and foremost in a relationship, which starts now on earth with God. God's radical plan is about redeeming relationships and love is the tool for reconciliation that flows through us.

"If you keep my commandments, you will abide in my love ..."
John 15:10a

Jesus is not so much threatening to remove His love if we disobey as much as He is clarifying the natural order of life. Love comes from God. God is looking for obedient conduits through which He can reach the world. We do not originate love; we pass it on. In other words, we cannot continue to love without obedient connection with Him first. To love is to obey so we remain in God's love when we love others.

Over the years, the Lord has loved me through people around me. One summer in college, I worked at an outdoor camp. Dave, the camp director, was one of those people. He was tall and goofy and full of life. That summer, he took the time to get to know me personally. He called me aside to listen, encourage me and give me bow and arrow lessons so my team could win the staff competition.

I was humbled and encouraged because Dave's investment in me was not compulsory. He did not have to go out of his way for me. He saw the potential inside me. Though Dave was my boss, that did not stop him from getting to know me and spending time with me. In no way did our relationship contradict his position as my leader. It strengthened it. I wanted to follow Dave because he cared about me. He could have used his time for many of the jobs he had to get done for the camp, but he made it a priority to be a fisher. The confidence he gave me could only have happened if he chose to give up other activities to spend time with me.

Love and time go hand in hand. If we are to love like Jesus, we cannot love well without sacrificing time. We cannot fish for people and love our own time and agenda more than God's.

The joy of relationship

The Father, Son and Spirit are the great Pursuers, heroes and rescuers of relationships. Jesus did not fish alone and He does not expect us to. He worked in relationship with Father and Spirit in a collaborative, missional effort. If you want to know how much God loves us, consider how far Christ moved to come to earth and die on a cross. Love requires the sacrifice of coming to people and the measure of love is how far we go to be with someone.

So why does God pursue us with sacrificial love? The answer, I think, is joy. Joy is relational delight. It is on outcome of love and happens during our pursuit of people. God is joyful in pursuing intimacy because of His relational nature. Jesus was joyful in His pursuit because of the joy that of relationship with the Father and the joy people give Him. There is an indestructible joy between the Father, Son and Spirit. This joy grounded Christ's mission and it was joy that caused Christ to pursue others.

> *"If you keep my commandments, you will abide in my love, just as I have kept my Father's commandments and abide in his love. These things I have spoken to you, that my joy may be in you, and that your joy may be full. This is my commandment, that you love one another as I have loved you."*
> *John 15:10-12*

Jesus makes a connection between His love and joy. When disciples remain in God's love their joy will be complete. Joy flows from loving relationship.

Joy is our soul's response to love. Like electricity running through a lightbulb, joy lights in us when love runs through us. Humans are conductors that illuminate God's joyful life when His love energizes us. We are like lightbulbs, which glow to display God's radiance. As lightbulbs need both an intake of electricity and outlet, we need to receive and release love flowing through us. Likewise, some Christians miss God's joy when they fail to receive God's love or fail to pass it on.

Joy is relational, not situational. Referring to after the resurrection, Jesus said to His disciples, "... I will see you again, and your hearts will rejoice, and no one will take your joy from you" (John 16:22b). When they beheld the risen Savior, they would know that He would always be with them and their source of joy will be eternal. King David said that God filled him with joy in His presence (Ps. 16:11). So, if we want to experience the joyful presence of God then we need to be moving and walking where He is going. Our world has tried to convince us that joy is a result of indulgence, inward looking and stuffing ourselves with comforts. However, the joy we want actually comes at a sacrificial cost.

Joy is a litmus test of whether we are doing life and ministry with God. When we follow Jesus' way, our joy lightbulb lights up and we glow God's radiance. We do not need to literally see God in order to have this joy. The apostle Peter said, "Though you have not seen him, you love him. Though you do not now see him, you believe in him and rejoice with joy that is inexpressible and filled with glory" (1 Pet. 1:8). Joy is an indicator of the health of our relationships too. It is true in marriage, in friendship and with our children. The more we love and serve others, the healthier we are and the more joy fills our relationships.

Co-laboring in ministry brings us joy, not just because of the purpose but because of the friendship with Jesus along the way. If we find ourselves with a lack of joy, we must examine our motivation and methods. Jesus' way is hard, but not impossible and it is the hope of joy that motivates us.

In serving, Jesus' joy becomes our motivation and strength. We do not wait for the strength to go out and do it, for it is in the doing that we find joy for strength. We will not run dry because God's love for people does not run dry. We will always find purpose in pursuing people because there is not a person on earth that God does not want to love and pursue.

Joy reveals our joyful God. Without joy, people are less likely to listen. When a child sees a commercial on TV or sees a friend with a new toy, what makes them want it? It is the smile on the child's face who has the toy. It is not just the toy that sells itself. It is the expression of the "user" that makes others want it. True joy is obvious to others. It cannot be faked and therefore it is one of the greatest "marketing" tools in evangelism.

When we try to serve without joy, it looks fraudulent, faked and not genuine. It actually contradicts our message and testimony. People know when something is truly joyful and life-giving. When Christians stop pursuing people like Jesus, it not a coincidence when they lose their joy. Burnout comes quickly when people make ministry a relation-less task.

My wife worked at a home for abandoned babies. After work, I would come and visit the home and spend time with the kids. I grew fond of one of the young children, Benjamin. I will never forget one day when I came into the home. I opened the door and we locked eyes. He was on the other side of the room with toys in his hands. As soon as he saw me, he smiled, dropped the toys and ran straight towards me with a huge grin on his face. My wife and the other staff watched speechless. His expression of love was profound. I opened my arms and picked him up. You can imagine in that moment my heart was full of joy.

Like with Benjamin, our heart's and God's are filled with joy when we run to Him in love. That is why Christians should be the most joyful people on earth. Jesus used the word "joy" seven times in the Passover discourse with His disciples, indicating the perfect joy we experience when we know and follow Him. The closer we are with people, the more joy we experience. Intimacy brings joy to God and it is God's joy in us that shines when we pursue people.

Material competition

A rich young ruler came to visit Jesus one time. He thought he was good enough, but his grip would not let go of his material possessions. Jesus offered him relationship, but he could not walk away from his riches.

From our perspective, we know that the relationship was worth far more than any riches. Yet, many Christians wander from God's design for life and ministry and fail to choose the path of pursuing relationships. We see this worldly mindset when programs supersede relationships, attendance is more important than transformation and efficiency and visibility are more important than obedience.

The world is not in need of money, buildings or programs. The world is in need of obedient disciples who pursue people with God's love.

One of my favorite church services was on the side of a hill in South Asia. I was there helping after a recent earthquake. A church near where I was working had been in a building before the earthquake, but the walls were then cracked. Since there were still residual tremors, the church decided to meet outside the village on the side of a hill. As people slowly arrived, we took seats in the dirt. Our worship was simple and beautiful as we sat on the side of that hill. There was one guitar, no stage, no formal program. That moment was just as worshipful, if not more, than any service I have attended in a building that holds 1,000 people.

Perhaps with Jesus' people-first strategy we don't need as much as we think we do. We can be fishers anywhere there are people. Jesus did not have a building, organization or even a home to call His own, yet He loved more than anyone in history. When we put things before people, we have believed the lie that money is in short demand. Actually, we are in desperate need of deep life-changing relationships. The world does not need our wallets, it needs God's presence.

We need to get our priorities right. There is, and never will be, a short cut for loving people. Relationships are the context for bearing fruit. That does not mean that money should be avoided. Once we get the priority right, we find that money can have an important role to play.

> "I tell you, use worldly wealth to gain friends for yourselves, so that when it is gone, you will be welcomed into eternal dwellings." Luke 16:9 NIV

Money can help us love and grow in relationships. It has a role, but it is secondary to the greater work of relationships. Do not just give people material things on earth. Give people the opportunity to know the Eternal One, gaining the gift of eternity.

The temporal serves the eternal. Thus, money must serve relationships, not the other way around. When money is invested into relationships, it becomes an eternal investment, bearing the fruit of love and generosity. That is far better than any stock market! That is why Paul was adamant to raise money for the poor in Jerusalem (2 Cor. 8:1-15) and the apostle John said that God's love should compel us to share material possessions (1 John 3:17).

I met a missionary who was often asked for money. His response was, "I only give to people I know." He was not saying "no," but rather clarifying what the point of money is for. The door was open still, but it required a relationship first. Of course, many beggars did not want that and walked away because they only wanted money. They correctly realized that forming relationships are harder than making money. Money is to serve relationships, not the other way around. When we get it right, we will reveal God through the fruit of love and generosity.

Made for Friendship

"Greater love has no one than this, that someone lay down his life for his friends. You are my friends if you do what I command you. No longer do I call you servants, for the servant does not know what his master is doing; but I have called you friends, for all that I have heard from my Father I have made known to you."
John 15:13–15

Jesus' words are nothing less than staggering. He pursued humanity all the way from heaven to the cross and He wanted to go even further. He took precious time to clarify how valuable His disciples were. They were more than servants; they were His missional friends.

Jesus did not say, "Greater love has no one than this, that someone lay down his life for a stranger." You may think that love is best expressed to complete strangers. You've likely seen a movie along those lines. However, it seems according to Christ, that love is best expressed in a more intimate relationship. How can we love someone deeply whom we do not know?

Similarly, Jesus did not say, "Greater love has no one than this, that someone lay down his life for a servant" for a servant does not have the same intimate relationship that is shared between friends. Jesus has a common mission with His disciples. Missionally, that makes them peers and colleagues.

Jesus knew the power of friendship to reveal and express love. A friendship with deep love has the potential to reveal that love in a tangible way. Friendship is able to demonstrate love because in friendship there is both affection and commitment. Temporary affection is not love. Commitment without affection is religion or duty. Love needs both affection and commitment and Jesus demonstrated both.

Jesus could have spent time sharing a detailed strategic plan to reach the world. Instead, Jesus wanted His disciples to know that, despite all their failures, relationship with them was His plan. They were His pursuit, joy, and delight all the way to the cross. He died for His friends for a reason. Through them, He would carry out His mission to reveal Himself and redeem humanity.

Though we might feel entitled to God's love, we must understand that we do not deserve Jesus' pursuit and friendship. We minimize the Gospel when we believe that God is saving a deserving people. God's purposes go far beyond us.

It is our small and often selfish view of the Gospel that causes us to fail to extend God's loving friendship to others. Salvation is not a pursuit of holiness where we compete to be on top. If anything, following Jesus is a path to the lowest seat at the table. It not random self-denial, it is intentional for the sake of the lost and our brothers and sisters around us.

The apostle Peter struggled with the idea of a humble and pursuing Lord. "You shall never wash my feet!" Peter said (John 13:8). Peter thought feet washing was too low for a king to stoop. What kind of king stoops to the dirt? Peter perceived that if his King went to the dirt then he would have to go at least as low.

We are not much different from Peter. We want a Gospel that saves us from a die-for-your-friend kind of love. We want a lofty king because we want our high place of recognition with him. When Jesus bent to His knees in John 13, He set a humble path for us all -- one we would rather not take in our flesh. We see the path in Jesus; response to Peter, "'If I do not wash you, you have no share with me'" (John 13:8b). If we chose Jesus as our king, our only path is to reciprocate His radical sacrificial friendship in the lives of others.

The "other" syndrome

It is amazing how quickly children make friends. My daughter can make a friend on the playground in a matter of minutes! Kids quickly bond over what they like to do, whether it is on the playground or at home. Yet, for some reason, many adults grow out of this mentality and struggle to form friendships as they get older.

The secret, which kids innately understand, is that friendships form over commonalities. As we get older, busier and our interests change, we stop using our friendship-making muscles. As mature Christians, we must re-learn this practice, adopt a child-like mentality and exercise these skills again. Friendship isn't for children; it is for fully formed disciples because it is a part of the nature of God.

Adults should have the advantage in making friendship because the more important something is, the deeper the bond we can form around it. Children bond over playing together. Christians should through our mutual pursuit of the glory of God. So, the question we must consider is, why we are not building friendships around the most important work on earth?

My son Coen has a friend with the same name, Coen. When they spend time together, my son often calls him, "the other Coen" as if "other" is a part of his name. We have tried to get him to stop adding "other" to his friend's name, but it seems impossible. What makes it funny is that his friend calls our son the "other Coen" as well!

This instinct to differentiate ourselves from others reminds me of a popular TV show, *Lost*, where passengers land on an isolated island. They eventually find out there are more people on the island and begin to refer to them as the "others." The drama unfolds as both groups try to navigate life on the same island with "other" people, different from them.

Deep down, we all struggle with the "other" syndrome. We see people and immediately want to differentiate ourselves from them. Our first reaction is to see differences between us, even though we are 99 percent similar. This tendency to separate and differentiate, if left unchecked, can lead to hatred, family disputes, church splits and global wars.

Our sinful nature pushes us to lean towards divisiveness. Our flesh urges us to be the king of our world. Since there can only be one king in each kingdom, we either compete for a kingdom or separate to reign supremely by ourselves. What results is a billion small, divided kingdoms that have little impact on the world, not to mention little love shown between the people in them.

Cain had the "other" syndrome. You can see his desire to be ruler of his world because, while Abel gave the very best sacrifice, Cain held back his best (Gen. 4:3-5). It seems that Cain wanted the best for himself and he hated that his offering did not compare with Abel's.

Hatred reveals that we do not see ourselves on the same team. Cain hated feeling second best. He hated that Abel was praised for his sacrifice and hated not being favored in that moment. God immediately warns Cain to be careful of the sin that could rule over him. Cain unfortunately acted in sinful anger and murdered Abel. God's punishment of Cain, interestingly, is to limit the fruit of Cain's labor and to make him a wanderer separated from his kin.

Sin separates. Satan has not just been separating people from God, he has been bringing division among all people, especially the people of God. Satan's "other" strategy prevails when we see everyone as on the "other" side. Notice how, in the garden, Satan tried to convince Eve that he was on her side and God was on the other side by implying that God did not have her best interest at heart. Satan wanted Eve to doubt what she was told (Gen. 3:1-5). Both of Eve's relationships, with God and with Adam, were damaged when she chose to sin. Likewise, Cain saw Abel as competition instead of as a brother. The list of people living with an "other" mindset goes on and on. It extends to include us, making people more isolated and our world more divided.

The blessing of diversity

Jesus offers a way forward that is unifying and compelling. He offers friendship to sinners and calls the Church to unite under His Lordship. Under the King, every friendship is a step towards kingdom unity. God's work is not about ignoring or eradicating the differences between people. His vision is to appreciate and unify those differences under Christ though friendship.

I grew up playing football (soccer) on an ethnically diverse team. We had Africans, Americans, Spanish and a Caribbean player. We had skillful inside players, tall and strong defenders, precise forwards and long-distance wing players.

If you asked the mostly Caucasian teams we played against, they would have called us the "other" team. Since teenage boys are not typically sensitive and understanding of other cultures and traditions, we were the brunt of many jokes. The jokes did not bother me too much because we usually won on the field!

When we got on the field and played, we were one team, united, driven to win, and there were few teams that could stop us. Our unity came from our common identity as a team and our common passion to win. Even though we had differences, the mission to win overcame them. In fact, within a common goal, diversity becomes incredibly valuable. We came to respect our differences as we united around what we shared in common.

The "other" mentality will thrive in the Church if we want to receive the glory, be on top, get the credit and pursue our own goals apart from others. We see this with churches and ministries filled with people who fail to see that they are on the same team. It is "their" program, "their" resources and "their" team. All else is considered "other."

However, division will quickly dissipate when we have a common identity and mission. The only identity and mission strong enough for such large-scale unity between people of different ethnicities, socio-economic backgrounds and political views is found in Jesus and His work. He alone can call people from every nation, tribe and tongue. He alone can give a mission compelling enough to require all types of gifts and personalities. He alone can inspire love and unity among our brothers and sisters. He alone paves the way forward in the type of deep, meaningful friendships where both diversity and unity are celebrated.

Relearning friendship

Friendship has the potential to unify the diverse global Church in an unprecedented way. Unfortunately, friendship is an uncommon topic from the pulpit. It floats in the air like a piece of dust: always there but never looked at directly. Sadly, Christians have let the world define friendship. As my friend Alexey said, "We need to relearn friendship from Jesus."[6] To relearn friendship, we need to look at three categories, starting with the one that founded the universe.

1. Friendship within the Trinity. Before the foundation of the universe, God existed. He is pre-existent and self-sustaining. Before atoms, particles, light and the world as we know it existed, God was. His foundational identity is "I Am" because He simply exists without the help of anything else. He needs nothing and His existence is the reason for ours. He is the originator of all life. He has no needs and fulfills all needs. It is impossible for us to comprehend because we are created, finite and limited by our mental capacity.

God is three persons perfectly unified as one God. God is three distinct beings who communicate and interact with each other. Thus, God is fully and perfectly relational in nature. Father, Son and Spirit coexist in a union that is impossible to parcel. They were together before creation and together involved in the work of creation.

From our human perspective, there is certainly mystery within the Trinity. We are not given every details or complete understanding and we do not need to. The Scriptures do reveal what we need to know. In several places, like in John 13-17, we get a glimpse of this relationship when Jesus talks extensively about the Father and Spirit. It is clear that Father, Son and Spirit speak to each other, listen and act and move in perfect harmony, relating in love, and out of love, accomplishing a common loving mission.

We get enough of a glimpse of the Trinity to know that it supersedes anything else in creation. We see the intimacy and value for one another in the words of Christ when He says, "And now, Father, glorify me in your own presence with the glory that I had with you before the world existed" (John 17:5). There is a glory about the Trinity where each Person shares in the fullness of majesty.

We often think of love as an emotion or something we do. Love leads to those things, but love first flows from Someone. The apostle John said, "God is love" (1 John 4:16). That verse does not say God is loving, it says God is love. Love flows out from the only source of love, God. The persons of the Trinity relate to one another, understand and serve one another in selfless, flawless, passionate and joyful love.

This love, God's love, flowed into creation. Perhaps the love of God was so vast it needed to be expressed in a new way, like a gift from and for the Trinity. Galaxies, particles, trees, planets, turtles and humans were formed out of a divine expression of love. Creation was and is an expression and context for love.

In the same way that God's loving nature brought forth creation, it is the loving nature of God that motivates His redemptive plan. It is the love of God that allows for the restoration of all He has made because His love has both affection for that which He made and commitment to that which is best for it. Being all powerful, He need not abandon that which He created and adores.

When God made us in His image, He deposited something valuable in us that is worth recovering. It is our mark of the divine that makes us worth recovering, capable of being friends. Perhaps it is His image in us that motivated God to rescue us, not only for our sake, but for His too. This identity, and God's desire to recover humanity, are due to his relational and loving Triune nature.

Father, Son and Spirit work together for this common goal of redemption because they are committed to love. The plan is loving and the way it is carried out is in perfect love. It is the Father who sent Jesus. It is the Spirit of God who empowered Christ to be born in the virgin Mary and came upon Christ at His baptism. Jesus carried out the plan of salvation, offering His life to the Father on our behalf. Through Christ, the Spirit came upon the Church to administer the power of Christ unto the saints. All were, and still are, involved at every step as the story continues.

Within the Trinity, Jesus takes a position of humility and dependence. Jesus called God "Father" and asks us to do the same because the Trinity chooses to be known and understood in this relational way. Jesus never resisted or struggled with His role. In fact, it was this foundational relationship with the Father that allowed Christ to walk in confidence despite the misunderstanding, desertion and persecution of men. Jesus confidently obeyed the Father and gave the Father credit for the miracles, words and plans He carried out. Jesus said, "I glorified you on earth, having accomplished the work that you gave me to do" (John 17:4). In the garden of Gethsemane, Jesus intimately lays down His will for the Father's, committing His death into the Father's hands.

This cosmic relationship in the Godhead provides us a foundational perspective for why we exist. It grounds the grand narrative of creation and our lives. This means that creation and redemption include humanity, but it is not solely about humanity. We come into God's story, but are not the center of it. And, if we are called into this story, then we cannot live well without loving and we cannot love without God. Hence, we are fully dependent on God and on His perfect Triune love. We can only look to it, depend on it, learn from it and model it.

2. Friendship between God and you. Fortunately, we find

ourselves as the beneficiaries of God's divine love. The apostle Paul says that the mystery of the universe is that Christ would live in us (Col. 1:26-27). The enormous love of the Trinity actually propels salvation on earth for mankind, which is why we claim no special merit for our salvation. We are both observers and beneficiaries of God's Triune love.

God's love could have remained solely within the Trinity. Instead, His love flowed out and allowed for our redemption. Jesus said, "I have manifested your name to the people whom you gave me out of the world. Yours they were, and you gave them to me, and they have kept your word" (John 17:6). The way that God talks about His people is like a treasure. We were the Father's, whom Jesus found like lost sheep and purchased on the cross and are given as a gift. Therefore, we come into God's story like a precious gem that reveals His worth and significance.

Only a triune God that has been loving from eternity past could write such a beautiful redemption story. For this reason, the Gospel message stands alone, and against, every other ideology, philosophy and human religion. Jesus opens the door for us to not just observe love, but participate in it.

When Jesus talks about eternal life, it is not about a destination but rather a relationship. Knowing the Father means far more than we can imagine. To know the Father and Son is to know eternal life (John 17:3) because life flows only from God, the origin of life. Therefore, our eternal life begins when we enter into communion with the eternal Father, Son and Spirit. With this gift, we have the privilege of asking of the Father and He will give us whatever we ask in the name of Jesus (John 16:23). This is the privilege only for sons and daughters of the Most High, those who are friends with Jesus and ask in His name. Since the Father has already approved the will and plans of Jesus, we can confidently pray in faith for it.

The story demands our participation. Our friendship with Jesus depends on it. How could we be friends with a perfectly loving God and not go and love others? There are no barriers left in our love for others. Jesus already came to us and became the way to the Father (John 14:6) who loves us and wants us to approach Him and ask of Him (John 16:26-27). And, we need to ask because we have a mission to participate in.

3. Friendship between you and others.

"Beloved, if God so loved us, we also ought to love one another."
1 John 4:11

The implication of the Gospel expressed in this verse could not be clearer. The apostle John, addressing his brothers and sisters as "friends," says that we are to love others because God loved us. God's invitation into loving friendship is not about joining a privileged club with God. It is about joining Him in service, in a great rescue mission that demands our lives.

God's love, poured into us through His Spirit, cannot end with us. We are meant to be vessels through which God wants to reach the whole world. If we fail to share God's love with others, we are like closed circuits, dirty fish tanks, stale lakes. We have everything inside us, ready to be poured out. Yet, we refuse to pass it on.

The Gospel is an invitation into radical love, which is why our friendship with Christ requires sacrifice. If we are committed to loving people in a broken world, we cannot love without giving up our time, resources and personal agenda for the sake of others. God's benevolent love fights for His beloved children and works for their good (Rom. 8:28) and bring freedom (2 Corin. 3:17). We must do the same.

When I moved away from home for college, I was away from family and friends. I did not have the support and relationships I had growing up. Early on, I struggled to find friends. I had rarely been in a situation before where I had to pursue friends. The Lord used a fellow student to teach me about friendship. He pursued friendship with me. He was intentional to spend time with me, introduce me to his friends and invite me on trips. Through that friendship, I felt God's love and pursuit and it taught me how to do the same for others.

Later that year I remember walking through a sports hall on campus. I stopped and noticed someone playing basketball alone. The Spirit prompted me and I was compelled to reach out to that stranger. Though I resisted the prompting initially, the burden grew until I walked over to him. Through that conversation, the stranger became a friend, got connected to Christian fellowship, began following Jesus and even helped lead a campus ministry a few years later. As I look back, I can humbly see that the Lord had initiated that encounter and invited me into an opportunity to love someone on His behalf.

God is pursuing us and calling us to pursue others. There are people all around us, divinely placed in our lives so we can participate with God in His mission. Our friends, family, neighbors and colleagues are not so by accident. They are divinely placed in our lives so God can reach them through us.

We love like Jesus because, as Paul says, Christ's love compels us (2 Corin. 5:14). God's love cannot be contained in us. If His love is for people in the whole world, then it is too large for just us. It will naturally overflow out of us and into the lives of others. And, if we are faithful to Jesus' example, this love will compel us into friendship with those God has placed in our path.

In John 4, Jesus pursued a woman at a well. When the woman realized that Jesus offers eternal life, she went to tell others (John 4:39). Though it was a short dialogue, she quickly understood God's heart and intention to love and save all people. Christ's love for her could not be contained. It compelled her to be a missionary to her people.

The more we grow in friendship with Christ, the more we join Him in mission by loving those He puts in our path. These friendships must not end with us. They too need a missional outlet. Our Christ-centered friendships are an onramp into engaging His world and co-laboring with Christ to redeem humanity.

Make it Missional

When I was a boy, I went through a phase where I loved firetrucks. One year, my parents planned a birthday party for me at a fire station. My friends came and we had cake and presents. As the birthday boy, I got a chance to ride in the firetruck with the firefighters. But when my parents took me to the firetruck, I did not get in. I was too scared. I cried and did not want to leave my parents. My parents tried and tried to persuade me, but I never got in the firetruck. I had loved firetrucks and had been so eager for the party, but when it came to the best part, I missed the opportunity.

Like my love for firetrucks, many people love the idea of God's mission. They understand it and talk about it with their friends. They have maps on their walls and globes in their office to remind them of God's work around the world. But, when the chance comes to get in and go, many people do not. They would rather stick with what they know than go.

For this reason, I fear that many Christians are not meaningfully engaged in God's redemptive plan on earth. We talk about missions like it is optional instead of the driving force behind the Church. God's mission is not something to just be given lip service. It is not something to simply observe. It is not adventure or cultural curiosity. It is the pursuit of people for the glory of God. It is a lifestyle that demands we leave the familiar behind.

It is no wonder Christians in church are wandering and unmotivated. We have lost our vision for the joy and excitement of doing relational ministry with Jesus. We will not fully appreciate and enjoy God's Church without its mission, which is the purpose meant to help fuel the Church. That is why the

Church often feels like a bus stop instead of a rocket ship.

Jesus has set the destination and provided all the fuel we need. His mandate is to make disciples in every nation, *ethne*, meaning culturally-unique people group. That means that wherever we are, our work cannot just reside within our own fellowship buildings or cultural boundaries. We must reach outside our comfortable cultures.

It is estimated that there are more than 17,000 people groups on earth with a unique culture and language. Of those, there are more than 4,500 ethnic groups, making up a fourth of the world's population, that are fewer than .1% Christian and have "no evidence of a self-sustaining gospel movement."[7]

God's work is not finished. While these statistics may seem enormous, insurmountable and impossible, the point is not to overwhelm you. They are a reminder that God still has good works He wants to do and we are the means He uses. Jesus could have stayed and done the work by Himself. Instead, He gave the Church the Great Commission as a wonderful invitation to partner with Him.

Opposition to the mission

The world will oppose God's work and agenda through any means possible. Today in secular society, the work of evangelism, outreach and disciple-making is being fought as modern culture becomes increasingly hostile towards people with a "religious" agenda. Countries are closing their borders to missionaries and Hollywood often portrays Christian's as antiquated, controlling or insecure.

The narrative that only Christians or religious people have an agenda is false. In reality, knowingly or unknowingly, everyone has an agenda. Agenda comes from our perceived needs. For example, if we were hungry, finding food would be an agenda. When we are lonely, finding a companion can be an agenda. When a person is without God, finding satisfaction apart from God will be their agenda.

Need is not the problem; humans are needy. The problem is where we seek to meet our needs. Only in God can our needs be fully met with overflowing love. Because people desperately need God, His loving agenda is to save and redeem people. God's love compelled Him to come to earth to save us (John 3:16). He did not wait for us to request help. He proactively moved in our best interest to meet our spiritual need.

Jesus' friends must adopt His mission. We cannot water down His agenda and we cannot pretend the world is fine. If we remain lukewarm about God's mission, eventually the Spirit will convict us like the church in Laodicea (Rev. 3:14-19). So, if we are going to get on the firetruck with Jesus, we need to face the reality that our agenda, God's agenda, demands service and sacrifice.

This is why the apostle Paul tells Titus, "And let our people learn to devote themselves to good works, so as to help cases of urgent need, and not be unfruitful" (Titus 3:14). God's redeeming work must lead us into good work, helping those in need. The Gospel demands fruitfulness and this fruitfulness does not come accidentally. It demands our intentionality.

Fortunately, this is not something we do alone. God's mission is for the whole Church. This is why friendship is so foundational to God's mission. It is one of God's greatest tools to faithfully respond to the life-saving mission at hand.

One big sinking ship

Imagine you are on a large cruise ship and you happen to visit the bottom level and notice a major leak in the hull. Water is coming into the ship and it will sink if the issues is not addressed. At this point, you are the only one that knows about it. Truth has changed your perspective and no matter what other pressing things you have going on, your new priority is to get everyone safely off the ship. You will either try to save people or not, but you cannot be without an agenda at this point.

The proper loving agenda would be to tell people about the leak and help as many of them as you can off the boat and into safety. Now, think of the world's advice: "Don't bother people with your agenda. Keep it to yourself. It is all the same, keep your opinion to yourself!" This worldly "wisdom" may sound good with the pretense of keeping peace, but it is based on ignorance. Apathy is a selfish agenda. If the boat is sinking, then inaction is unloving. Ignoring reality cannot bring peace in the long-term.

Above deck, everyone is carrying on as normal. No one is waiting around for a message that disrupts their plans. Boldness, awkwardness and interruption may be required. That does not mean that we should be unwise. Paul also said, "Let your speech always be gracious, seasoned with salt, so that you may know how you ought to answer each person" (Col. 4:6). Paul was bold, but he was not foolish.

After discovering the leak, it would be wise to find a few people, probably the first people you run into, and tell them. Since you cannot force people onto rafts, all you can do is passionately speak and act, hoping they believe. But certainly, out of love, you would not just tell them to jump in the raft and wait. You would tell them to tell others. Is this sounding like Jesus' strategy?

You could also make an announcement over the speaker system. That would likely have some results, but it could also create havoc and confusion. Some would believe you. Some would help others. Some would run to the life raft and trample people. And some would not believe it, thinking it was a prank (unfounded truth). Some personal follow up would be necessary to "disciple" those people who had just heard the message over the speaker system. Nothing validates our sincerity better than interacting with lost people face to face.

If you just tell them the ship is sinking, that does not bring a lot of hope. You would want to tell them the exit strategy. You would point people to the life rafts. Specifically, you would want to tell them how to get to the life rafts, how to use them and how to shepherd others who were there.

Jesus is the only hope in our sinking world. Our job is not just to tell people they are going to hell (though that is a message God wants people to hear, especially for those that do not believe the boat is actually sinking). Most of the time, we need a bit more tact and wisdom. We need to explain why the ship is sinking and what they can do to live. If they respond with faith in Jesus, then we need to train them to pass the same good news on to others. The world may call that an inconvenient and pushy agenda, but God calls it love.

Two by two

One of God's brilliant world-saving strategies is fellowship. As mentioned in a previous chapter, in 2017, I was sent to Turks and Caicos to help with hurricane relief. When I arrived, the organization paired me with a colleague from London. Our job was to mobilize the churches on the main island of Provo to deliver necessary supplies for those who had been affected by the hurricane. We had access to supplies, but we needed to lay the groundwork for distributing material first.

We had a generous local contact on the island who was willing to host us, help us, lend us a car and give us food to eat. Our biggest blessings often come in the form of people. Through our local contact, we met a pastor who got us connected with other pastors on the island. In a few days, we were mobilizing dozens of churches and preparing for the supplies to get offloaded from the planes and distributed through the churches. You know about one site that did not go well, but overall the distributions went so well other large aid agencies were asking us if they could use the churches as their distribution sites!

*"Two are better than one, because they
have a good reward for their toil."*
Ecclesiastes 4:9

This is timeless truth and Jesus took it seriously. We usually think about teams for accountability, but they are also important for our effectiveness and our witness. As Solomon said, two are better than one, for one can help the other if they fall, they can also strengthen, defend, and remain strong together (Ecc. 4:9-12). Two people are not just two times as effective as one person, they are three, four, or five times as effective.

Jesus sent out the 12 disciples and the 72 in pairs saying, "The harvest is plentiful, but the laborers are few" (Luke 10:2a). It is interesting that if the workers are few, would not it be wiser to spread the workers into individuals instead of teams? Jesus does not do that, however, teaching us that two is a wise minimum for an effective missionary force.

There may be two people, but that does not make them independent from God's help. As Jesus is sending them out, he tells them to pray for the "Therefore pray earnestly to the Lord of the harvest to send out laborers into His harvest" (Luke 10:2b). Prayer, inviting God's presence, is still necessary for teams. The heart of the prayer is for God to multiply labors and efforts for the Father's harvest.

It is not a coincidence that Jesus sends His disciples out in two's and tells them that He is sending them like lambs among wolves (Luke 10:3). We need fellowship because we are in for a difficult task. The world will not love our message. Two is not enough to be a majority, but it is enough to be a voice in difficult times. There will be retaliation and persecution. A strong missional friendship can help deal with this reality. It provides both prevention of pride in successes and safeguard from discouragement in isolation in rejection.

Jesus gives some counterintuitive instructions. The pairs are not to carry money, bags or sandals. Should not fellowship allow them to be independent? No, the teams are not a strategy for self-sufficiency. They are still to trust the "Lord of the harvest" in everything, even for their basic provisions.

They are told not to greet strangers on the way. I do not

think this is for their safety. I think it is about focus. They are called to a specific village of people. When you have a heart or calling for specific people, other people can be the biggest distraction from those we are supposed to minister to.

When the pairs get to their destination, they are not done relying on God. They must trust God will provide a person of peace, a home for them to stay at and food to eat. Perhaps discerning the person of peace takes two people. It was not just about trusting God to bring converts. It was about building faith at every step. This kind of faith required a companion to refresh and encourage along the way like Paul and Silas who were able to pray and sing together in jail.

Dependence and reliance on people is a strategy. It demonstrates what kind of people they were and what kind of God they followed. They were proof to the new village that the God of the missionaries is a Provider. It was a way to attract listeners. Dependence also provides an opportunity for others to be engaged in ministry alongside the pair. The needs of the missionary pair were an invitation for that person of peace and others to engage in ministry by tangibly contributing to the missionaries' needs. It was an open invitation to the work of God.

Healthy, God-centered relationships, are like a magnet of love and service that attracts others to join. When the missionary companions came to villages, they preached, healed and proclaimed. But the disciples also interacted with each other. People were watching the way they made decisions and talked to each other, how they submitted to and loved each other. This display of Gospel-compelled love synchronized with their proclamation of the Gospel.

We know the disciples carried on this strategy of going two by two. Paul goes with Barnabas on one of the first missionary journeys. Even when Paul and Barnabas split, they both take someone else with them, showing they were committed to the model of serving in teams. We know in Paul's letters that he built many missional friends along the way, mentioning many by name. In his letter to the Romans, Paul greets 24 people by name. This is not to mention the households he greeted, the people he indirectly mentioned and the people he sent greetings from! He didn't just list names either. He cared for them deeply and called them "co-workers" (Rom. 16:3) and "dear friend" (Rom 16:9). Similarly, the apostle John, who lived the longest, signed off his last letter, "The friends greet you. Greet the friends, each by name" (3 John 15b). Perhaps he had so many friends at that point that he could not even list them all!

With Jesus, Paul and John, it seems clear that their friendship included missional engagement. Their relationships were not just for personal enjoyment or self-serving. They knew their mission would be difficult, if not fruitless without others by their side. They understood that God uniquely designed friendship and missions to go together and I believe there are three main reasons for this.

1. Mission brings friendship

Mission is for God's glory, and it is also for our growth. Friendship fuels mission and mission fuels friendship. When Jesus called the disciples, they responded to a personal call. Their intent was to follow Jesus, but what they ended up with was a band of brothers for the rest of their lives. Likewise, as we walk with Him, we naturally get closer to others who are close to Him.

Imagine, after finding the leak on the cruise ship, that you put together a rescue team to save the passengers. You work hard, plan and do everything you can together. You are eventually safe on shore after the incident, seeing the fruit from hundreds of people saved. Would those rescue team relationships feel cheap or shallow? Of course not! The mission was not fraudulent, it was life-changing. Working together breeds love, sacrifice and respect between the missional coworkers, the very ingredients for friendship. This same effect happens in wartime situations, business ventures and certainly in ministry.

When people come together with a common commitment to God's purposes, the relational bond that forms is a powerful testimony to the world. It shows that God's plan unifies people. Jonathan and David had this kind of common purpose. God's path led David to the royal courts where he met Jonathan. We know they had respect and affection for each other, but they also had a common passion for God's will in Israel.

The principle for us is to walk on mission with God and see who He brings beside us. Years ago, I longed for deeper missional friendship. I asked the Lord for colleagues in my generation who were on mission, running for the Gospel, anywhere in the world. Around that time, I was invited to a global gathering of younger leaders in southeast Asia. It was an answer to prayer.

Leading up to the event, I served on the prayer team with Josh. We helped facilitate prayer before and during the event. Working together allowed us to get to know each other and we built trust through a common heart for prayer and global mission. When we finally met each other in-person with the other leaders, it was like we had been friends for a while.

Many of those relationships on the leadership team have continued. In 2019, we spent time together to catch up, encourage each other, pray and worship. We shared hurts and needs. We prayed and listened to God for each other. It was a time of refreshment and friendship with each other and the Lord.

This is the brilliance of God. When we go on mission with Him, He brings us into fellowship along the way. So, when we come together around God, the depth of that friendship is as meaningful as the work He calls us to.

2. Mission propels friendship

Mission brings people together, but what about those we are already in relationship with? What about those we have known for years but never had any meaningful missional engagement with? Generally, friendship without an ongoing purpose becomes selfish or fades away. Conversely, it thrives with purpose. The right mission will propel, lead and guide friendship in a healthy way.

We can learn from Jesus. He may have known about the disciples before He called them into ministry, but at some point, He made a clear call for them to follow Him completely and leave their lives behind. We cannot lead people to Jesus secretly. At some point, we must make a clear call for people to join us on mission.

A while back, I was setting up a trip to Atlanta to grow my team of financial partners. I needed to ask a friend there to help connect me with donors. I was a bit sheepish about asking, but he knew what I needed when I asked. He confidently replied, "Of course I would love to! We have a missional friendship." I was honored, but I had to eat my own words about confidently asking because of my hesitation.

Let us be confident in our asking and giving amongst friends when the aim is God's mission and glory. Mission does not cheapen relationships, it bonds them. Mission keeps friendships healthy and makes it not just about us. It is about serving. When we walk together towards God, we naturally grow closer to each other.

For our current friendships, we may need to refocus their purpose. If a relationship exists between believers in Christ without any progress towards becoming like Christ or serving Christ, then it is not missional. The mission does not cheapen the relationship, it dignifies it through the dignity of the mission. Jesus is calling us into what we were made for and He is the relational glue.

We were made for good works in the context of relationships. Jesus gives us an identity that is meant to be active in the world. Thus, we must be near people, not only so we can learn who we are, but also for us to put our gifts into action through service. And, when we invite people into mission, we are inviting them into their calling and purpose. We are also inviting them into a deeper relationship with us and God.

When we stifle the mission behind friendship, we are limiting our calling, our friendship and our fulfillment. Jesus calls us not because He needs our help, but because He loves us. He wants to be with us along the path as much as He wants to reach the destination. The world is longing for friendship and looking for the ingredients, ingredients that God has already given us if we will be obedient.

3. Mission requires friendship

We cannot fulfill Jesus' mission without friendship. Jesus' plan requires making disciples and Jesus showed that friendship and discipleship go hand in hand. Part of being a disciple of Jesus is to being a missional friend of Jesus. After someone becomes a disciple of Jesus he or she then goes and makes other disciples, who become missional friends. Therefore, missional friendship is part of discipleship. If Jesus felt it necessary to become friends with His disciples for the sake of mission, then we have no other pattern to follow.

We live in a lone ranger mission culture. When we work in isolation, we ignore God's mighty relational tools for bearing fruit. We do not need someone next to us at every moment, but we should act in unison.

Jesus says to "love one another," and to "make disciples in all nations." These are not contradictory or competing commands. They are two sides of the same coin. Love is both missional and relational. Love has a godly agenda and desires intimacy. Missional friendship is where loving relationship and directional discipleship come together. To be missional is to love and to lead people into the apprenticeship of Christ.

To disciple people and not invite them into mission is contradictory. In discipleship, "participation" is often the forgotten "-tion." Participation is about mission. It is a response to justification, part of our sanctification and prepares us for glorification.

Discipleship is not something we "lord" over people (Matt. 20:25-26, 1 Pet. 5:3), it is about walking alongside them. We cannot trick, force, coerce or intimidate people into becoming disciples. We make disciples through love. Loving people like God makes people want to be more like God.

God will change people and He wants to use us to do it. We participate through our love towards people both in action and in the truth we speak. Paul says, "If I give away all I have, and if I deliver up my body to be burned, but have not love, I gain nothing" (1 Corin. 13:3). Our best mission efforts gain nothing unless they are done in love, an overflow of God's love in us.

Loving discipleship is the only kind of true discipleship. Jesus perfected the coalition of relationship and direction, discipleship and love. The reason is that a relationship is uniquely capable of helping someone learn and grow.

Change is more than informational; it is also relational. This means that discipleship does not have to be programmatic, formulaic or formal. It can happen in just about any context. A meal can be as life-changing as a mission trip.

Wanderers, walkers and warriors

The practical question is, who will we go on mission with? I think it is important to qualify the kind of people we can serve alongside and I think there are three main categories of Christians to choose from. The first group are the wanderers. Wanderers know the Lord, but they are likely new, confused or stagnant in their faith. They are not walking in the direction God has for them. They are like plants with no roots. Wanderers have little truth to follow straight, so we should engage them in the way a teacher guides a student.

The second group are the walkers. Walkers may know God's mission, but they are slowly making their way towards it. Their biggest challenge is apathy and distraction from the world. They are like plants with shallow roots. Since we are not on the same field, we should engage them like a sports coach spurring on players to run harder.

While pursuing Jesus means traveling alongside these first two groups, there is a third group of people that is essential to fruitfulness. These are the people who bear 30, 60 or 100 times what is sown. They are "running with perseverance" and "fighting the good fight." They do not have to be perfect, but they know their identity in Christ, their calling and they are running that way. They are warriors for Christ.

Warriors are on mission. Paul exhorts Timothy to, "Flee the evil desires of youth and pursue righteousness, faith, love and peace, along with those who call on the Lord out of a pure heart" (2 Tim. 2:22). The Greek word for pursue gives the impression of extreme effort and focus. If we are running with God, we must come alongside those who also have a pure heart, which comes from clarity of purpose.

Who are the warriors that God is putting around you? Who is relentlessly on mission that you know and respect? Will you invite them to serve with you, running in such a way as to get the prize (1 Corin. 9:24)? If you are wondering whether any warriors are around you, wait and trust. Run to Jesus. He brings friends alongside us. The closer we are to Jesus, the closer we are to His people. Eventually, as we run, we will bump shoulders with great warriors as we crowd around the throne.

Filling gaps

When God puts missional friendships around us, where do we begin? Since there are countless needs around us and in the world, the first step is to ask the Lord of the Harvest. He knows far better than we do. If His words remain in us, then ask and it will be given that we bear fruit for His glory.

There is never just two people serving together. "For where two or three are gathered in my name, there am I among them" (Matt. 18:20). Missional friendship is, at least, a team of three with God and God is the great binder and unifier of relationships. As we walk with Lord in friendship, our question is, "Lord, what are you doing and how can we join?"

In college, my friends and I had a burden to start a Christian outreach club. We felt the Christian community needed a way to tangibly serve the community. That year, the Lord brought together an incredible team of believers who were passionate about practical and loving service.

We began to meet, pray and discuss when and how we could serve. One snowy day, we gathered people to shovel snow for those who needed help in the community. I will never forget the response of one lady we helped. She cried with joy when she saw us shoveling her snow. Through our service together was simple, I know she felt the love of God that day.

Once we understand God's vision, we can identify the gaps and prayerfully consider if and how we can fill them. On the way, may find missional gaps where people are moving the wrong direction, perhaps building the wrong kind of "kingdom." Or, we may see relational gaps where there is a lack of unity and intimacy.

Our response to both gaps is the same. We are called to build loving friendships and encourage greater engagement in the good works God has prepared for us. This mission requires the Church to come together. We do not need to know every Christian or work with every Christian, but we do need to be walking in the same direction together, unified around the One who calls us.

SECTION 3

Friendship Collaboration: The Kingdom of Jesus

Thy Kingdom Come (Unity in Mission)

There once was a wise king who brought peace to the land. He wanted an heir to his throne so he organized a competition. It was a several-day race through a vast forest. The winner would become the heir and next king. The people knew their warrior king was brave and cunning so they expected a difficult course. All the young competitors trained their hardest, choosing the wisest and fiercest warriors to prepare them.

The race was complicated and grueling. Some competitors got lost. Some ran out of supplies and some gave up. Finally, after many days, two men came walking towards the finish line, shoulder to shoulder. The bells announced the coming competitors and the crowds roared with excitement. When the two came to the stage, the organizer asked them, "How did you do it?" They replied, "We did it together."

One of the finalists took off his hood and revealed himself to be the king. The king stepped on the stage and congratulated other competitor saying, "In wisdom and humility you invited me and followed my lead. You are ready to rule and worthy to inherit the kingdom."

As Christians, we are on a path towards God's fully established kingdom. How foolish we would be to get to the end and realize that we could have walked with the King the entire time. We were never meant to go through life and ministry alone. Our King knows the way. Why would we not follow Him?

The King's path

"And behold, I am with you always, to the end of the age."

The short story above clarifies an important and often neglected truth. Future heirs of the kingdom do so much achieve the kingdom as they do receive the kingdom. Christ is the rightful King over heaven and earth and He will usher in the full Kingdom. Our self-reliant efforts cannot build the kingdom. Instead, in and through Christ, we receive the kingdom as an inheritance as rightful heirs who walk with the King.

The narrative of the Bible points to the One who has already overcome the world (John 16:33). Jesus walked perfectly with the Father and fulfilled God's work (John 17:4). Jesus, reigning now, has authority on heaven and on earth (John 17:2) and is reclaiming the dominion that humanity lost.

That means that our efforts on earth are not to be victorious alone, but point to the victorious One. Since we are not of the world (John 17:14), Jesus commissions us in the world as His representatives (John 17:18) in order to point the watching world to Him. He gets the spotlight on the podium, but willingly shares that with us, His victorious Church.

Our journey is a collaborative effort where our best efforts are sanctified and energized through His Spirit working in us. Eternal life, which is fellowship with God (John 17:3) equips us for the path which is challenging and treacherous. His presence brings both protection from the evil one (John 17:11, 15) and sanctification through His Word (John 17:8, 14, 17). This sanctification has a missional purpose. It is not just about becoming better people. It is about being better vessels who bear fruit and reveal God with us. Like being fit for a race, sanctification is about missional fitness. Sanctification is about becoming like Christ, who ran perfectly, and perfectly fulfilled the Father's plans.

This puts a new light on fellowship, which has a destination and missional purpose as well. Unity happens naturally when we run to the same destination together, knowing that those we run with are a part of the kingdom we are running towards.

The fellowship creates a testimony larger than just one person and also provides a vehicle to accomplish the larger task. As the African proverb goes, "If you want to go fast, go alone. If you want to go far, go together."[8] The unity that Jesus desires (John 17:11, 23) is not just about going to the same place, it is also about going together to make the Father known (John 17:24).

Investing in an eternal foundation

Missional friendship is about running towards the kingdom in fellowship. When this genuine and heartfelt fellowship becomes the DNA of our life, we capture the bigger vision of bringing God's kingdom to earth. We must be careful to remember that we are not building our kingdom, we are reflecting and conforming to His kingdom.

> *"nor will they say, 'Look, here it is!' or 'There!' for behold, the kingdom of God is in the midst of you."*
> *Luke 17:21*

The kingdom is near when the King is near and kingdom citizens have the presence of the King. Thus, the kingdom grows as people enter into relationship with the King and His people. Since this is a kingdom that will last forever (Luke 1:33) our relational efforts are invaluable because they are built on an eternal foundation.

The work of unity is far from complete. Josh, a prayer and worship leader in Southeast Asia, says, "We know each other in church about as well as people know each other in a movie theater."[9] This is a sad truth. The bricks in our churches are far more unified than the people inside. If we are going to change, we must focus on the relational reality of the kingdom. We must shift from seeing the bricks to seeing the people and from mortar to relationships. Though kingdom relationships are hard to see and measure, we know and trust that God is growing that foundation.

In 2007, I was on the campus of Virginia Tech in Blacksburg, Virginia when a gunman killed 32 students in dorms and classrooms. I woke up that morning to the news, confusion and panic, wondering what had happened and if my friends had survived. It was tragic for all of us young college students who had never encountered death so closely. The school decided to allow students to end the semester early and go home if they wanted. However, many of the Christians intentionally decided to stay on campus to minister to the students who remained. During those weeks, the Gospel was proclaimed to the broken and lost.

I remember during that time that a few Christians planned to gather in the center of the campus on the large open drill field to pray. Our group met, held hands and closed our eyes to pray. We earnestly prayed for healing and God to move. After some time, to my astonishment, when I opened my eyes the circle had grown significantly. While we prayed, people walked by and joined.

This is a picture of God building His kingdom. Even in tragedy, He is using His people, united around Him and seeking His kingdom first (Matt. 6:33), to grow a kingdom at His initiative. When we gather around Him, the potential is endless both in witness and work. Our small steps of reliance, humility and prayer make a visible impact on those watching, which the Holy Spirit uses to draw people in.

We are a city on a hill. We are an enigma to the world, as we show physical and practical unity around the invisible God. We cannot hide and the world cannot ignore us. Any time we gather in Jesus' name, it causes others to consider the kingdom, like a foundation that points to a magnificent structure being built- a kingdom from every nation.

"After this I looked, and behold, a great multitude that no one could number, from every nation, from all tribes and peoples and languages, standing before the throne and before the Lamb, clothed in white robes, with palm branches in their hands,"

God will establish His kingdom of saints, redeemed from every nation, tribe and people on earth. In Revelation, we see a kingdom that is carries a unique dichotomy of both inspired diversity and perfect unity. There is diversity among cultures, unified around Christ the Lamb. This unity-among-diversity is intentional and central to our work because it proves Christ's unsurmountable wonder, worth and weight.

Inspired diversity

A strong building needs diverse materials, efforts and expertise. It is no different with God's kingdom. He wants a diverse people who are unified in community and working together. Kingdom diversity reveals God's attractiveness and vastness and helps accomplish the mission to glorify God.

At the tower of Babel, people strove for unity apart from God and apart from His inspired diversity. Interestingly, Babel unity came from a vision to build a magnificent structure. God destroyed that mission because it was not centered on Him or His purposes.

God's mission is more compelling and unifying than Babel. His mission reverses the curse of the Tower of Babel. Christ's kingdom finishes the story and unifies the scattered saints. Now, in and around Christ, the saints from each nation can gather in His kingdom. This kingdom-unifying mission is too big for any one person or culture, so we need diverse people, relationships and gifts to accomplish God's work and reveal His unimaginable nature and magnificent glory.

Community, by nature, is diverse. It includes a range of differences between those from various backgrounds. This is the goal of Christ's kingdom and it is healthy for the Church now. Thus, we must seek diversity and learn to appreciate it, not just for our sake but for the glory it brings God. Diversity makes the foundation of the kingdom stronger. Diversity reflects the vastness and grandeur of God, who reigns over it all. The more diverse the Kingdom is, the more glory God receives when it is brought together and unified under Him.

In order for kingdom diversity to be possible, the shared value and commonality, in this case a love for the King, of the community must be deeper than the backgrounds people come from. This is possible when people who are united in Christ come together in and through friendship, which overcomes cultural differences. In godly friendship, this common unity in Christ is the focus, not the differences.

Kingdom culture doesn't erode diversity; it celebrates it. When God reveals Himself to an ethnic group, their praise is unique for they see and experience God in a different way. When those diverse saints come together, it gives God greater honor with unique worship harmoniously blended. False gods are limited by culture, time and space. Our God attracts the worship of billions of people with unique DNA and culture.

The universe stands in awe of the sheer beauty of our Lord who receives worship from every nation. Nothing else can demand this kind of attention from every square inch of creation. One day, as we stand around the throne and look around at the diversity before the King, we will be amazed at the captivating nature of God. Each culture will help us see God in a new way like a collage and inspire new worship in our hearts.

Perfect unity

The unity Jesus prayed for (John 17:20-21) is possible because of Jesus. There are two aspects to this unity: 1) spiritual and 2) functional. Our spiritual unity comes from our shared identity, truths and beliefs in Christ.

"eager to maintain the unity of the Spirit in the bond of peace. There is one body and one Spirit—just as you were called to the one hope that belongs to your call—

one Lord, one faith, one baptism, one God and Father
of all, who is over all and through all and in all."
Ephesians 4:3-6

In Christ, we share the same Spirit, body, hope, faith, baptism, God and Father. This is the glue that brings the Church together in a world-defying way. This spiritual unity is possible for every believer everywhere, whether we meet each other or not. In Christ, we are spiritually bound.

This spiritual unity leads us to common mission and worship. Church diversity puts God on display when it comes together around Christ. And, as diversity increases, so does the display of Christ-centered, world-shocking unity. It is our hope of perfect unity and the glory of the kingdom to come that motivates our efforts. These are not easy efforts. To unify around Christ is to move against the grain of the world. It requires service that comes at great sacrifice to ourselves, but our motivation is for the King more than ourselves. His desire for unity must take precedence over our comfort. It is for this reason we must love Christ more than our own lives, for we must love the unifying object of our affection more than ourselves or we will grow stale in our quest to unity.

On the path to Christ, we also grow in functional unity. Our shared beliefs lead us to action. The focus moves off of ourselves and on to God. We trust in His provision, not the worlds. We seek His approval, not the worlds. We love others instead of ourselves. This is love in action.

This is why the blessing of spiritual unity comes with a responsibility. We need to feel the ownership and connection of what we share. The same Spirit who unifies also empowers the Church to love and serve. The Spirit brings gifts that are intentional, beautiful and perfectly fit for the task at hand. Functional unity is a lifestyle of practical service. As Jesus said, how we love one another is the defining mark of His disciples (John 13:35). And, it is so important that when Christ returns, He will separate the sheep and goats based on how we loved and served those in the Church who are in need (Matt. 25:31-46).

God's economy of gifts and needs

> *"Behold, how good and pleasant it is*
> *when brothers dwell in unity!"*
> Psalm 133:1

Functionally, God has set up the Church to operate in love by providing us, broken and needy people, with divine gifts. This ecosystem of gifts and needs creates an atmosphere where we can both serve and be served. The Spirit's gifts match the needs and when the gifts meet the needs, God is put on display.

Several years ago, I went with a team to bike through part of South Africa. I was one of the weaker bikers in the group and struggled at times. At one point, I was lagging further and further behind. It felt pointless to try and catch up, but our guide, Mark, slowed down and dropped back to where I was. He essentially said, "Just watch and follow me." He positioned his bike right in front of me and my eyes remained fixed on his back tire. Within minutes, I looked up and we had caught back up with the group.

God wants His community to move together, but we all need motivation, encouragement and guidance at times. The Church is meant to be a supportive missional community like this. Our gifts have a missional purpose and expression to help others get to where we are going. For the community to move effectively, we need experts of all kinds. Our strengths and weaknesses affirm our dependence on God and give us purpose within relationships. This is God's economy, His structural design causing His people to come together and give Him glory.

Like a bicycle team that rotates positions to maximize efficiency, we need others to come alongside those who are lagging behind and use their gifts in order to keep the group together. The Holy Spirit, our perfect guide, is the One who equips and empowers people to come alongside other people. He provides gifts to serve and prompts our motivation to serve others. Often, He uses people around us to be an encouragement to lead us back into community and back on track.

> *"So neither he who plants nor he who waters is any-*
> *thing, but only God who gives the growth."*
> *1 Corinthians 3:7*

There is no room for pride in the Church. Pride is counterproductive to unity. Our gifts and roles are not about us, but about God who is expressing Himself through us. God has made His people a community where no one has everything, so that the Provider over it all is made known.

God's economy consists of gifts and needs and that shapes our kingdom culture. It challenges the selfish to be givers and the self-supported to be receivers. Love is the practical and tangible currency of the kingdom. For example, when my wife is sick, her increased needs are an opportunity for me to step in to cook and clean more. The opportunity allows me to express my love for her tangibly.

Since gifts and needs are given at God's discretion, we can find joy in our gifts and needs. As a missionary, I raise support. My family depends monthly on the financial donations of friends and family. Over time, I have come to appreciate this way of living as I have understood God's economy. When people give to us, they are showing tangible acts of love. Meeting our financial need may seem like a simple transaction, but it is also more than that. It is a spiritual act of friendship and community when it is done out of love for the glory of God, sowing in His Church. As we know, love and mission grow friendships so you can imagine how much closer we are with those who lovingly sacrifice for us financially each month.

Needs are for God's glory and the sanctification of the Church, so do not keep your needs or gifts to yourself. When God brought Israel out of Egypt, He told the Levites they would not have land, a physical inheritance or fields for income. He wanted them to be dependent on Him and others for a reason and through that encourage their trust in Him and the generosity of the other tribes. It was no coincidence that the spiritual leaders of Israel, the Levite priests, were supposed to be the most dependent. To meet the need of the Levite priests, the other tribes of Israel needed to sacrifice their portions regularly. Israel offered their first fruits to God as a spiritual act. As they did so, their sacrifices tangibly provided for the needs of the Levites.

This economy requires real sacrifice. Fortunately, God has already shown us how. In the sending of His Son to die for our sins, He modeled for us the sacrifice we should display with each other. He started community and entered into it with us when He saw our need, our sinful state, and sacrificed by sending His Son. We enter into relationship with God when we trust Christ as our Savior and we then follow Christ's example by loving and serving as He loved and served us.

Needs allow love to be manifest. Paul's experience that he shares in Philippians 4 displays an example of this when he thanks the Philippians for sharing in his need, providing for him financially. Paul clarifies that he is content in Christ, so it is more about the act of giving than it is the gift that is given. Paul says, "not that I seek the gift, but I seek the fruit that increases to your credit" (Phil 4:17). Paul says he and the Philippian church entered into a special partnership of giving and receiving (Phil 4:15).

The world is full of gaps, needs and broken relationship bridges. God has allowed this so that He can be seen and glorified in our response to those needs. Gaps are opportunities for God to be manifest through us when we love people as He first loved us.

Meeting a need can be carried out across great distances and cultures. Paul saw the financial needs in Jerusalem as an opportunity for the Gentile church to love their brothers and sisters and in doing so make God seen. Paul said, "As we carry out this act of grace that is being ministered by us, for the glory of the Lord himself and to show our good will" (2 Cor. 8:19b). Paul said their act of generosity pointed to God and imitates Christ's generosity to us (2 Cor. 8:9). The distance of giving from the Gentiles was not a hindrance to the giving; it actually magnified the generosity.

Paul asked that the money be given willingly, not under compulsion (2 Cor. 9:5, 7), given as an act of love not one of obligation, which is how God loves. We can give our bodies to the flame, but without love it does not glorify God. Love comes from Him so our actions must flow from His love inside us. Love is the manifestation of God in and through us. Selfish sacrifice is not love. It must be in union with God and communion with others, like a friend that lays down his life for another (John 15:13). Without love, we are like the Pharisees who followed the letter of the law but did not have love for God in their hearts. They gave their tithe, but neglected the greater things of love (Luke 11:42).

In God's economy, it's less about the amount of the gift and more about the love in which we give it. God does not need anything. He has all the resources in the world. He could make money appear out of thin air or a coin in a fish's mouth. God chooses to use us and so has ordained good works in advance for us to do (Eph. 2:10).

God's brilliant strategy brings us together in Christ-exalting unity. When we give away our small amount, it is like the fish and the loaves. Our little act of love can go as far as God wants it. In community, the generosity of one person has exponential impact that inspires others to sacrifice. One transaction in the kingdom can inspire thousands more and greatly impact the surrounding culture. The question for us is, do we understand the significance of the opportunities around us? Do we know our gifts? The greater the need around us, the greater the amount of sacrifice that will be required to meet it. The greater the sacrifice, the better the opportunity to show God's love and experience His joy and intimacy in community.

Christ-honoring cross-cultural friendship is counter-cultural. It requires giving and receiving regardless of location. A loving community, close in proximity or not, will bind the gaps and bridge the canyons so that God's love is visible to the searching world. The Church then becomes a light of fruitful and functional relationships that is foreign to the world. It is attractive and breathtaking when done well. It makes outsiders stop, think and wonder, "Where does that love come from?" We see a glimpse of this in the early church in Acts 2:42-47. As Christians gathered in fellowship, they met each other's needs and God brought more people into the church.

Likewise, today, when the world sees the unity of the Church through physical acts of love, it opens the door for evangelistic conversations and for more people to be saved. The world will see the Church as an attractive anomaly, a "city on a hill," forged by beautiful friendships that forces the lost world to wonder and walk towards God's brilliant light in us. This is the kingdom culture to which God wants to bring the lost into. The question is, do we live in such a way, relationally and sacrificially, so that the world will see God in our interactions?

Practices for Next Generation Leaders

The world is not in a shortage of needs, but there is a shortage of people who know how to respond like Jesus. The Church need to renew its vision and passion for friendship that bears fruit Jesus' way. If we want to see King Jesus exalted in every nation, we have to follow His strategy.

I hope and pray that the next generation of Christian leaders will commit to change and prune away practices that are not bearing fruit no matter how hard it may be. This begins with a new perspective, new values and new behavior. So, as we consider doing ministry Jesus' way, let me propose a few foundational shifts that we can begin with.

Abiding before leading

Leadership has become a seductive term. Culture often exalts leaders and so people want it without knowing why. They are drawn to the power and image it brings, but this was not the path of Christ. We must resist this kind of leadership and redefine the term, and praxis of it, biblically.

Jesus always led from a place of abiding. He set the example for us of a human being who lived in perfect relationship with God the Father. What we observe in the life of Jesus is the perfect expression of both isolated abiding and active abiding. By isolated abiding I mean spending time alone with God, in solitude and reflection. By active abiding I mean communing with the Almighty God and hearing and respond to Him throughout everyday life.

We tend to talk more about isolated abiding or oversimplify the two, like isolated abiding is about hearing and active is about doing. Both require trust, listening and obeying. Both have a time and purpose in bearing fruit. Isolated abiding is not just for those who have nothing to do. It is essential for those busy in ministry and foundational to being more effective with less. Active abiding is part of the Christian life too. Active abiding entails walking with God into chaotic crowds with complete confidence. Active abiding combines poignant teaching with acts of physical service. It causes us to share the Gospel in one way in one situation and an entirely different way in the next, based on the specific people involved and God's leading in the moment (see the example of Jesus in John 3 and 4).

No matter the circumstance, our challenge is to keep an abiding relationship with Jesus first in our hearts and habits. When we rest in God's authority and power, we have no need to seek our own. Abiding in Christ should end our wandering and striving for worldly significance. We can do nothing a part from Him so He must work through us. Our perspective, therefore, is not about position and placement but about obedience and fruitfulness.

To abide well in the quiet and loud, fast and slow, chaotic and predictable, requires an understanding of spiritual rhythms. Like Jesus, we need times of resting and running, waiting and walking.

For leaders who struggle to slow down, we must sit at God's feet before we can effectively engage the world. The world will not freely offer us time with God. We must relentlessly simplify, rest and renew in Him, away from distraction and temptation.

Leaders lead *best* when they are the first to *rest*. God rested after He created the universe. One way leaders lead is by avoiding unnecessary activity. The temptation of worldly leadership is to focus almost exclusively on getting things done, on being physically and visibly productive. Our tendency to overcommit and overwork often comes from a lack of abiding.

Christian leaders can rest because the mission is God's, not ours. To sit and be still is one of the most counter-cultural things we can do, especially as the person who is supposed to lead, make decisions and keep moving. Jesus went out of His way to be quiet and listen to His Father. It was His intimate moment in the garden that filled Him with strength for the cross (Matt. 26:36-46). This kind of abiding is rare and the world needs to see more Christians who live it out well.

Abiding leaders live like they can do nothing without their King. Prayer is essential. And, if prayer is not required, the mission may be too small. My friend Josh says there are two main ingredients for prayer: urgency and intimacy. We need urgency because faithfulness happens in a given time and space. We do not have forever. We need intimacy because our hearts sacrifice for what we love. We must know and long for time with our Lord. Intimacy requires time. Abiding leaders know prayer is never a waste of time, but is instead the foundation for a fruitful life.

For example, part of leading is selecting leaders to raise up. We often pick leaders for their resume, ideas, strategic thinking and/or ability to accomplish tasks. What did Jesus do before He picked the 12 apostles? He spent time alone with the Father (Luke 6:12-13). We must be open to God's leading and then be willing to engage future leaders in relationship to build trust.

For leaders who struggle to invite God into their everyday life, it is not just a matter of scheduling more quiet times. It is a perspective issue. It is a matter of not segregating God to the quiet portions of life. God moves in every aspect and seeks to redeem every aspect of life like our work and family. We must invite Him to life, move and speak in those areas.

People before programs

Making disciples in all nations is an enormous task, but we need not be overwhelmed. Jesus has given us everything we need to accomplish His work with Him. Too often, in a state of panic, we rush into worldly quick-fixes and human strategies to deal with our fear and uncertainty. As we have seen, the Great Commission is a relational process more than a programmatic task. God is redeeming a people for Himself and He works through His already redeemed people. Thus, relationships change people and the love we demonstrate is for the sake of the lost and for God's renown.

How we go about fulfilling the Great Commission matters. Programs, though helpful, are not where we should begin because they are off-center if the goal is results without, or regardless of, relationship. Relationships are the main method and result that God wants. To try to accomplish the mission apart from relationships is to misunderstand the mission. Relationships are God's primary strategy because people are made in the image of *God*, not *programs*. If people are the most valuable thing God has created then we should value and steward our relationships as our most important asset.

Fruit glorifies God and fruit comes through relationships. Programs alone do not bear fruit; the relationships in programs bear fruit. In other words, an organization does not lead someone to Christ, the people in the organization do. People do come to know about Jesus through billboards, television shows and radio programs, but people are still involved in the process. Information can be shared without a relationship, but we should be careful to give credit to God's people for the work of sharing information, not a "program." How we talk about people and programs reflects our theology. Programs are not made in the image of God, nor will structures and positions transfer into eternity. What does carry on forever are people, relationships and the fruit that we bear. The information, projects and programs we use are tools to lead people into relationship with God and other people.

We must see our work as primarily relational, not transactional. When we see the Gospel (a story and message) as transactional, our ministry will follow suit. God's work is relational and ours must be too. Programs should exist to foster relationships, strengthen relationship, build new relationships, give people confidence to share Jesus more, or help the relationship move on mission. Programs should never exist just for programs' sake because God is not counting programs, He wants fruit.

We should not see relationships as transactional either. It is not a simple system of input that always bears fruit. That is why, I think, Paul says that we can give our body to the flames without love and gain nothing (I Cor. 13:13). Relationships are not doors to enter into the room of bearing fruit. We do not pass through relationships for something greater. They are the room in which we dwell, enjoy, bless and are blessed by. Relationships are the house and friendship is the table we sit at.

When systems and structures serve relationships, they become powerful tools for God's work. That means that programs are accountable to people, and therefore running a program should never be an excuse for avoiding relationship. There is no substitute for the hard work of pursuing people because persevering love follows in the footsteps of Jesus. Which of these phrases honors people more? "I am in this program and need to help you." Or, "I want to serve you, how can I help?"

When Jesus sent out the disciples, He did so in the context of a training program. His instructions had a goal, destination and guidelines. Godly programs should be the same today. Godly programs foster obedience, community, love for the lost and dependence on God. Does a program create a place and space for God to move? If so, it could be a great tool and place for God to move and bear fruit. On the other side, problems arise when keeping the program running supersedes the purpose for which it was created.

For those who work cross-culturally, relationships are even more important. My friend Emmanuel, an evangelist in Africa, says the following about mission that is carried out through friendships:

> "Friendship has been a foundation of the African way of doing evangelism. With limited financial resources to run evangelistic missions, believers share what they

have during outreach events. People will feed local evangelists and mission volunteers and avail their accommodations, not only because of the passion of the lost but also, they were motivated by that missional friendship.

"Unfortunately, missional friendship is something that our generation is losing in working together with the global north and global south. God's mission has been become more project-contract oriented. People connect for a kingdom project but nothing else. I think that it's the reason behind the use of the term "Partners in Missions" rather than "Friends in Missions." A friend in African context is someone that you share your life with, someone that you value, someone you consider in your conversation, someone that you speak into his/her life, someone that you know beyond any other interests. This friendship goes beyond the two of you. It reaches your children and spouse.

"Missional friendship is needed for the emerging Christian leaders to advance the kingdom of God. When I visit the US, I feel at home because of the missional friendships I have developed throughout my journey in ministry there. However, when people come to Africa, I wonder 'Why do we host our friends from the west in hotels, not in our homes, when they are here in Africa for evangelistic missions?'"[10]

Friendship has the power to overcome a lot of cultural differences. Unfortunately, Christians often want to partner in work but not in life. I was convicted of this myself when staying with one of my colleagues in South Africa. As I was leaving, I said something like, "It's a privilege to work with you." His loving response challenged my mindset. He said, "We are not partners, we are family." It minimizes our work and the Gospel when we see our missional colleagues as merely transactional partners.

Do we see our Christian brothers and sisters as close as family? Larry Warren, a long-term missionary, has made it his ambition to be in close proximity to those Jesus mentioned in Matthew 25: the hungry, the thirsty, the stranger, the unclothed, the sick and the prisoners. If we do not know them, how can we love and serve them? The suffering church needs friendship and encouragement. We will see them in eternity. It would be wise to prioritize those relationships now, for their sake and for the sake of our witness to the world.

Leaders pursue people. We often think of leaders as the ones who are pursued, but Christ-like leaders are the ones who do the pursuing. It is tiring, which is why we must first abide before we lead.

Leaders must demonstrate the pursuit of people in every aspect of life: family, friendships and community. That means beyond just their vocational ministry hours. When ministry leaders fail to pursue people outside their paid positions, it discourages followers from everyday obedience that follows suite. In other words, pursuing people is a calling for all our lives, all the time, just as fruit is not born only through formal ministry.

Kingdom before kingdoms

Without genuine relationships, there will not be genuine collaboration. Unfortunately, many Christians are so focused on the mission that they see no room for deep relationships that lead to God-honoring collaboration. Those who fail to connect and collaborate are often living for their own small kingdom instead of Christ's. If our purpose in life is glorifying God, then we must seek the kingdom for the kingdom is where God is most glorified.

"Your Kingdom come, your will be done."

Matthew 6:10 NIV

Jesus taught His disciples to pray for God's kingdom to come. You cannot build Jesus' kingdom and your own at the same time. Leaders build their own kingdoms when they set off to change the world by themselves. Sometimes leaders do this out of pride and sometimes it develops out of an inability to work together with others. Not many Christian leaders intentionally set out with the goal of building their own kingdoms. Yet, many well-meaning Christian leaders end up there at the end of their lives with their own tiny kingdoms, proud of what they have done.

One time I had a call with a missions pastor who said he makes an effort to say "yes" to every possible effort for collaboration. I appreciated his heart of saying "yes" and being open to God's leading. Not every conversation will lead to collaboration, but it is important to have a posture of listening and looking for what God is doing. When we run fast straight ahead with our eyes down, we risk missing opportunities to collaborate for the glory of God.

Since God's glory is far beyond us, if we properly understand the task at hand, we realize that we cannot carry out the mission alone. Satan loves small kingdoms because they are easy to destroy. There is only one kingdom that will last: God's kingdom that He sent Jesus to establish. There may be room for small kingdoms now, but they are a waste of time. They will soon perish and we will regret every second we spent building them.

How do we know the difference between our kingdom and God's? It is the difference between a solo act and an orchestra, a life raft and a cruise ship, a backyard court and a championship stadium. God's kingdom work is far beyond what we can do because it is about His glory, not ours. So, we must ask, who initiated this work? What is motivating my work? Who is exalted, me or Jesus?

Human kingdoms are ones of convenience. Jesus' kingdom requires uncomfortable obedience. It is worth fighting for. We often justify disobedience in the name of creativity. Often it is just a way to avoid what we know we should do: the hard work of relationship-building and truth-speaking. Participating in God's kingdom will require us to go against the world and our old nature. It may require us to be confrontational, and turn the tables over of corrupted religious life. Or, it may call us to suffer for the sake of truth and non-compromising testimony to Jesus' Lordship.

Building God's kingdom requires that we release ownership. We fail to honor the Lord fully when we see programs as our own, both in our heart and how we communicate the work. We "create" programs, "lead" the work and can "run" them as we want. If we do not place structures, strategies or organizations under the lordship of Christ, we run the risk of building our own kingdoms. Putting our work under Christ means submitting to His Word and Spirit. This means obedience and there can be no obedience without knowledge of the Word and active prayerful abiding in the Spirit.

When leaders see the community they lead as "theirs," they often see themselves above the community they lead and fail to step into those communities. I heard about a church that did not want their leaders to attend that church because then the leaders would get too involved with the people. Perhaps they thought involvement would taint their ability to lead, but that is a far cry from how Jesus led His disciples!

A leader who nurtures community must see himself as a part of that community. Leadership is a function in the body, not superiority over it. Jesus alone is the head of the Body. If Jesus was willing to lead relationally and call His disciples friends, then Christian leaders should do the same.

If you see leadership as a seat on the top, you will isolate yourself and it is hard to lead like Jesus in isolation. People do not want to associate with that kind of leadership. Not to mention, it prevents leaders from building deep relationships, making real accountability impossible and leaders will not lead well without relational accountability.

As part of the universal body of Christ, leaders should also be willing to collaborate with other ministries, not compete with them. Collaboration starts with having the right perspective. If we view people as working for us, it is about our kingdom. If we view people as working with us, it is for Jesus' kingdom. Collaboration requires that we give up control. Collaboration happens when we come around one King. Conflict happens when the priorities of small kingdoms bump into each other. There is plenty of Great Commission work left on earth, God's glory has yet to fill the earth and God is not lacking the resources. We are lacking collaborative unity.

Collaboration happens one missional friendship at a time because the best collaboration begins with deep relationships. We collaborate when we use our God-given gifts in love. Knowing our strengths is not an issue of being proud. Instead, it is the avenue through which we best love others. If a strength we have is a God-given gift, it is likely accompanied by the perfume of joy. And there is no need to be threatened by believers with other gifts. In fact, if we are jars of clay who reveal God, then humility is our greatest strength. God uses most those who recognize their weaknesses. We should certainly know our gifts and how we can serve, but no gift is to be exalted above the others. Instead we should serve in unity with others around us. This kind of unity goes even further than just serving. It motivates us to suffer for one another, even unto death as Jesus showed.

Since leaders do not lead forever, there will eventually be transition. How those transitions go says a lot about the heart of the leaders coming and going and whose kingdom they are serving. We see a difference in leadership in the Old Testament between Saul and his son Jonathan. Saul resented David's future leadership, while Jonathan accepted it. Jonathan's view resulted in friendship, while Saul saw himself as an enemy of David. Today's Saul-like leaders create conflict wherever they travel. They are fearful of losing control. They splinter groups and cause division. They keep breaking off until it is just themselves that are left.

The world is watching how we lead and what we are living for. When we live for the larger kingdom of God, we will naturally lead in love with service the way Jesus demonstrated.

Our burden and path are "light"

Are you bearing fruit in life and ministry? All of us have room to improve. So, I hope, after reading this book, the Spirit has prompted changes in your life and ministry. Be prayerful and bold with those convictions. Seek council and commit to make the right choice even if it is difficult.

If you are not sure how to begin, just take one step. My dad was in the navy where a common saying is "it's easier to steer a ship that is moving." In other words, start moving in the direction God has revealed to you thus far. God does not need to give you every step at one time. Just take a step and wait for the next.

One of my favorite activities in college was to watch the sunrise from the top of a popular mountain nearby. Sometimes my friends and I would hike up right before dawn and other times we would camp overnight to make sure we did not miss it. When you have struggled to get to the top of the mountain, it makes the view more enjoyable and the journey worth it. There was something special about being on top of a mountain watching the sun come over the distant horizon, bouncing off of the clouds and spreading a blanket of warmth over the earth.

God's work is like the sunrise. God is not asking us to make the sun rise. He is not asking us to save the nations. That has already been set in motion through the raising of the Son. God will accomplish His plans, but He is asking us to hike with Him, bring others along and behold His glory.

Sadly, much of our participation is just watching the sunrise from our bedroom windows instead of climbing to watch it from the mountain top. If our hearts resist worship, we have not properly beheld Him. And, if those around us are not worshipping Him, it may be because we have not taken others along to see His glory on the mountain top. We are guides, but first we must be led by the risen Savior. Jesus reveals God's glory. As we follow Him, He reveals God's glory to us and then we get the privilege of taking others, in friendship, to behold it.

What a joy it will be when Christ returns and the saints gather before the throne. I hope in that moment, as we look around, we will see our closest friends on earth. We will see those with whom we labored, the one's with whom we climbed the mountain of God, the one's with whom we went through suffering, the one's with whom we baptized new believers, the one's who knew our families and the one's who knew our darkest pains and highest joys.

Our friendships will be enriched many times more in our eternal home, where there will be no barrier to intimacy with God or with others. The fruit of our labor will be clear as we see those we loved and served and who came to know Christ through our obedience. In that moment, we will know the joy of worshipping the Lamb with our closest missional friends.

> *Father, help us love you more than we love the world. Help us to know you more than we do now. Let us know your goodness, your love, your protection, your heart and your plans. May we learn to wait, to trust, to follow you well as we abide in you. May your joy overwhelm us in your presence. Lead us into loving pursuit of others so we can participation your redemptive work. Please give us a passion and vision for your Kingdom and destroy our small kingdoms. Raise up a generation of believers, pure in heart, who walk in mission and friendship for your glory!*

ENDNOTES

1   Dana L. Robert, "Cross-Cultural Friendship in the Creation of Twentieth-Century World Christianity," *International Bulletin of Mission Research International Bulletin of Missionary Research,* vol. 35, no. 2, (April 1, 2011): 100-107. https://doi.org/10.1177/239693931103500208.

2   Ibid.

3   From correspondence with Nana Yaw.

4   New International Version.

5   John Piper, www.desiringgod.org. This phrase is the slogan of Desiring God, a ministry based in Minneapolis, Minn.

6   From correspondence with Alexey, a friend of mine.

7   "Frontier Unreached Peoples," (2020): https://joshuaproject.net/frontier.

8   This phrase is widely recognized as an African proverb, but I could not find a specific source to cite.

9   From correspondence with Josh.

10 From Emmanuel Kwizera in an email sent on March 23, 2020.

Made in USA - Kendallville, IN
1238774_9781735482668
02.24.2021 0823